SEAMASTER 300 BRONZE GOLD

Loved by generations of adventurers, the Seamaster 300 represents one of the most famous timepieces in underwater history. Created in 1957, the original model was launched as OMEGA's first-ever professional divers' watch, featuring pioneering technical details that enhanced the safety of the diver.

Today, the legacy and timeless style of the Seamaster 300 lives on. Following a deep tradition of bronze craftsmanship at sea, the latest model has been made in OMEGA's exclusive Bronze Gold, an ingenious alloy that offers the warm aesthetic of bronze, yet with the luxurious inclusion of gold. Created for a soft pink hue and incomparable corrosion resistance, its precious colour and feel is truly unique.

To complement the Bronze Gold, OMEGA has given the design plenty of classic details, such as a dial fittingly crafted out of aged bronze, as well as open-Arabic numerals and a brown ceramic bezel ring with its diving scale in vintage Super-LumiNova.

As a Co-Axial Master Chronometer, the watch will require less servicing throughout its lifetime, while also guaranteeing the industry's highest standard of precision, performance and magnetic resistance up to 15,000 gauss, as certified by the Swiss Federal Institute of Metrology (METAS).

Ω
OMEGA

Bubble

Candle Holders

tf.design

THE
KINFOLK
ENTREPRENEUR
IDEAS for MEANINGFUL WORK
NATHAN WILLIAMS
THE KINFOLK
KINFOLK
TRAVEL
SLOWER WAYS to SEE THE WORLD
JOHN BURNS
All books are available to order at Kinfolk.com and wherever books are sold.

KINFOLK

MAGAZINE
—
EDITOR IN CHIEF John Clifford Burns
EDITOR Harriet Fitch Little
ART DIRECTOR Christian Møller Andersen
DESIGN DIRECTOR Alex Hunting
COPY EDITOR Rachel Holzman
FACT CHECKER Taahir Husain
DESIGN ASSISTANT Abbie Lilley

STUDIO
—
ADVERTISING, SALES & DISTRIBUTION DIRECTOR Edward Mannering
STUDIO & PROJECT MANAGER Susanne Buch Petersen
DESIGNER & ART DIRECTOR Staffan Sundström
DIGITAL MANAGER Cecilie Jegsen

—
CROSSWORD Mark Halpin
PUBLICATION DESIGN Alex Hunting Studio
COVER PHOTOGRAPH Michael Oliver Love

WORDS
—
Allyssia Alleyne
Alex Anderson
Lavender Au
Nana Biamah-Ofosu
Katie Calautti
Rachel Connolly
Ed Cumming
Stephanie d'Arc Taylor
Daphnée Denis
Tom Faber
Harriet Fitch Little
Bella Gladman
Robert Ito
Rebecca Liu
Nathan Ma
Jenna Mahale
Kyla Marshell
Okechukwu Nzelu
Mona Omar
John Ovans
Baya Simons
Apoorva Sripathi
George Upton
Pip Usher
Salome Wagaine
Annick Weber
Ryan Willms

STYLING, SET DESIGN, HAIR & MAKEUP
—
Nika Ambrožič
Dana Boyer
Michelle-Lee Collins
Laura Doardo
Andreas Frienholt
Louw Kotze
Natasha Newman-Thomas
Juan Camilo Rodríguez
Sommet Studio
Sandy Suffield
Nicole Wittman

ARTWORK & PHOTOGRAPHY
—
Oghalé Alex
Gustav Almestål
Sylvia Ballhause
Nick Ballón
Tine Bek
Sandra Berkovich
Max Bronner
Max Cavallari
Alexis Christodoulou
Justin Chung
Ruth Clark
Pelle Crépin
Bea De Giacomo
Marina Denisova
Tara Donovan
Daniel Dorsa
Camila Falquez
Lasse Fløde
Joe Horner
Cecilie Jegsen
Vicki King
Kourtney Kyung Smith
Romain Laprade
Laurence Leenaert
Rozenn Le Gall
Vicki Liang
Michael Oliver Love
Doan Ly
Oliver Mayhall
Katie McCurdy
Christian Møller Andersen
Zach Phan
Aaron Tilley

PUBLISHER
—
Chul-Joon Park

The views expressed in *Kinfolk* magazine are those of the respective contributors and are not necessarily shared by the company or its staff. *Kinfolk* (ISSN 2596-6154) is published quarterly by Ouur ApS, Amagertorv 14B, 2, 1160 Copenhagen, Denmark. Printed by Park Communications Ltd in London, United Kingdom. Color reproduction by Park Communications Ltd in London, United Kingdom. The US annual subscription price is $75 plus shipping. Airfreight and mailing in the USA by WN Shipping USA, 156-15, 146th Avenue, 2nd Floor, Jamaica, NY 11434, USA. Application to mail at periodicals postage prices is pending at Jamaica NY 11431. US Postmaster: Send address changes to *Kinfolk*, WN Shipping USA, 156-15, 146th Avenue, 2nd Floor, Jamaica, NY 11434, USA. Subscription records are maintained at Ouur ApS, Amagertorv 14B, 2, 1160 Copenhagen, Denmark. SUBSCRIBE: *Kinfolk* is published four times a year. To subscribe, visit kinfolk.com/subscribe or email us at info@kinfolk.com. CONTACT US: If you have questions or comments, please write to us at info@kinfolk.com. For advertising and partnership inquiries, get in touch at advertising@kinfolk.com.

HOUSE
FINN JU
finnjuhl.com

WELCOME
The Technology Issue

In 2001, the futurist Ray Kurzweil published an essay arguing that technology has ruptured the passage of time. "We won't experience 100 years of progress in the 21st century—it will be more like 20,000 years of progress," he wrote.

In this age of hyperaccelerated change, a technology-themed magazine risks becoming a relic before it's even hit the shelves. Rather than celebrating of-the-moment innovations, this issue of *Kinfolk* aims for some modicum of longevity by focusing on the systems and philosophies that underpin new technology, from the philosophy of Silicon Valley to the inscrutable laws of algorithms.

Our themed section begins with a profile of Anna Wiener, whose memoir *Uncanny Valley* details time spent among the egos shaping Big Tech. On page 157, we hear from a group of influencers who—with the assurance of anonymity—speak honestly about the good, bad and downright ridiculous aspects of living life for the 'gram. In our fashion editorial, photographer Michael Oliver Love envisions the point that Kurzweil believed the rapid acceleration of tech innovation would lead to: the singularity, the moment where technological change becomes uncontrollable and irreversible.

In Rage Against the Machine (p. 166), Tom Faber hosts a conversation with experts on algorithmic bias to better understand the hidden forces that shape what we experience online. "So much of public life happens on social media at the moment," says Dr. Carolina Are, a researcher and pole dancer who has experienced the murky world of Instagram censorship firsthand. "It becomes worrying how little we know," she says. It would be foolish to suggest that the solution to any of these issues is to switch off entirely. However, we hope the stories here help you better understand what we're plugging into.

Elsewhere, the magazine makes space for offline reflection. Dev Hynes—the hypertalented artist better known as Blood Orange—shares his perspective on stepping away when technology no longer serves you: "I just want to exist in the world," he tells Kyla Marshell on page 50. Our fashion editorial firmly pulls the plug and heads off grid for a weekend of camping in Spain. On page 104, Erchen Chang—London's bao superstar—creates gallery-worthy sculptures out of steamed dough, while on page 60, stylist and photographer Doan Ly has made gorgeous lamps out of gelatin.

If you're looking for a place to jump in, we would suggest you begin in the Starters section, where you'll find short essays on the cult of busyness, the meaning of dreams and how to craft the perfect out-of-office response.

The joys of tech notwithstanding, thank you for reading us in print. We hope you enjoy the issue.

WORDS
JOHN CLIFFORD BURNS
HARRIET FITCH LITTLE

Reseller in your region: stringfurniture.com/find-a-store
Born in 1949. Thousands of new combinations yet to be discovered.
string
String Shelving System waiting to be rediscovered. By set designer Hans Blomquist 2021.

CONTENTS

18 — 48

STARTERS
A serving of smart ideas.

50 — 112

FEATURES
Camping, Blood Orange and bao.

Photograph: Doan Ly

"The goal is just to see what I can do." (Dev Hynes – P. 54)

"I had the sense that there was nothing wrong with tech, but everything wrong with me." (Anna Wiener – P. 118)

114 — 176

TECHNOLOGY
A slow guide to fast systems.

178 — 192

DIRECTORY
Cult figures, codpieces and a crossword.

Photograph: Michael Oliver Love

18 — 48

CRAZY BUSY

There's no rest for the aspirational.

WORDS
REBECCA LIU
PHOTO
SANDRA BERKOVICH
/ LESYANEBO

There is a specter haunting modern life: the cult of busyness. Social schedules are stuffed to the brim; work has become the source of our identities; a smartphone ensures that we are only one alert away from taking ourselves out of the moment. And yet, hellish as this existence can be, is it possible that we *enjoy* bragging about our state of overwork?

In 2017, *The Atlantic* declared that "Ugh, I'm so busy" had become "the status symbol of our time."[1] It pointed to a recent study by US-based academics Silvia Bellezza, Neeru Paharia and Anat Keinan, who found that busy people are perceived as being "higher status"—a woman wearing a Bluetooth headset to conduct calls was seen as more important than one who wore headphones for music. This marks a huge reversal in how status is perceived. In the 19th century, aristocrats showed their power by emphasizing how *much* leisure time they had. Now, the researchers concluded, the rise of the knowledge economies, and the intense competition for jobs within them, means that those who boast about their busyness are asserting their status as (white-collar) workers in demand.

The same study found that busyness, when asserted by blue-collar workers, does not have a similar effect in boosting status. This is the ironic thing about the cult of busyness: It is the very people who need to cram their schedules to survive—gig workers, people with multiple jobs, parents juggling childcare—who are occluded from it. Those who are jostling for power within the rat race, proudly winnowing down their leisure time, tend to already be doing well.

Lockdowns around the globe during the COVID-19 pandemic prompted many people to recognize that the pace at which they were living was not sustainable. But has it ultimately released the power of busyness? A recent study showed that the average workweek across Austria, Canada, the US and UK has been extended by more than two hours a day since the pandemic began. If the past two years have shown us the importance of reclaiming our time, it has also made clear the need for a labor movement strong enough to enforce it. (It is no accident that busyness is particularly admired in countries with weaker employer protections; the same American study found that Italians believed those with more leisure time had greater social status.) The real solution to the cult of busyness, it seems, will not merely involve rejecting it psychologically; it feels, now more than ever, a question of worker power.

(1) The rise of the "side hustle"—an alternative source of income or accomplishment alongside regular working hours—has added to the pressure to forgo leisure time. A study conducted in the UK by Henley Business School found that people with side hustles work almost 13 more hours per week than the standard worker.

The act of conversation has always had an architectural framework. In ancient Rome, the triclinium—a small dining table surrounded on three sides by couches—was a dedicated space for food and talk. Chilly medieval houses added benches next to a central fireplace to create nooks for intimate conversations. Arts and Crafts designers in England and the United States adapted these "inglenooks" in late-19th-century cottages. As modern central heating made toasty alcoves unnecessary, 20th-century house planning blended functions across large continuous rooms. To make space for intimate talk in these sprawling open spaces, architects devised a novel (some might say novelty) solution: the conversation pit.

The Finnish-American architect Eero Saarinen, along with industrial designer Charles Eames, designed one of the first conversation pits in 1949 for publisher John Entenza. According to architectural historian Esther McCoy, writing in 1962, the living room in this house—Case Study House #9 in Pacific Palisades, California—"was designed on the principle of elastic space. . . which could graciously expand or contract for an occasional party of forty or a friend in for morning coffee." A lowered lounge area encouraged guests to talk while sitting casually against cushions on its carpeted steps.

Saarinen and interior designer Alexander Girard refined the idea further in a house for Xenia and Irwin Miller in Columbus, Indiana. In this widely published house, completed in 1957, a built-in couch and myriad colorful pillows surrounding the sunken conversation area softened and enlivened the stark white marble living room. Saarinen added a similarly colorful conversation pit under the fluid concrete vaults of the 1962 TWA terminal at JFK airport. Plush couches upholstered in crushed velvet invited travelers to lounge and chat as they waited to board their flights.

By the early 1960s, so many other mid-century architects had taken up the trend that a 1963 *Time* magazine article could claim derisively that "there was hardly a blueprint around that did not include specifications for a large, shallow hole to be sunk into the living-room floor." In arch terms it pointed out the potential "downfall" of this arrangement: Not only did the conversation pit separate out the smug and "more serious-minded" party guests who "could step down to form a sort of basement discussion group," it also put more frivolous guests in danger of tumbling down among them. "Today," the author claims, "few homebuilders are insisting on conversation pits, and a remedy has been found for homeowners discontented with the ones they have. A few cubic-yards of concrete and a couple of floor boards will do the trick."

The conversation pit idea has enjoyed a revival over the last few years, perhaps in the hope that architecture can help turn the attention of family members away from digital screens and back toward each other. But those same screens will, of course, contribute to the pits' precarity: Who hasn't stepped off a curb while scrolling on the move? Designers of contemporary conversation pits might be obliged to mar their sleek designs with a perimeter fence.

WORDS
ALEX ANDERSON
ARTWORK
ALEXIS CHRISTODOULOU

THE LOW-DOWN
An architectural conversation starter.

WORDS
KATIE CALAUTTI
PHOTO
VICKI LIANG

It is a truth universally acknowledged that inherent quotability keeps a novel alive in the public consciousness. But the nature of how we read has changed, as has the notoriety to which we assign quotations.

Historically, a quality literary quote contains elements of inspiration ("To thine own self be true"), advice ("It is nothing to die; it is dreadful not to live"), timelessness ("It was the best of times, it was the worst of times"), or a level of deeper meaning that underscores the readers' intelligence ("Time moves slowly, but passes quickly").

These esteemed turns of phrase were historically cherry-picked by critics and adopted into the culture over a span of many years. But the rise of e-book readers over the last decade has placed the lightning-fast ability to promote quotes in readers' hands.

The Amazon Kindle's open-source "popular highlights" feature allows readers to view an e-book's most highlighted passages and contribute their own. The result? Expressions memorialized through group think. One highlight leads to two, then 10, then 100—and a viral quote is born.

"Because sometimes things happen to people and they're not equipped to deal with them," in *The Hunger Games: Catching Fire*—one of the bestselling books of the last decade—has 31,072 highlights. If that many people consider it worthy of remembering, it *must* be good, right? The majority of popular highlights read not as beautifully written sayings, but like fridge magnet–style aphorisms.

Do literary quotations require gatekeepers, or is it inevitable that objectivity turns subjective when filtered through social tech? Perhaps a sense of quality is no longer required for a quote—instead, the act of annotating has become a way to connect with others during an otherwise solitary activity.

In an update last year, Kindle released a feature sure to take the self-curated quote phenomenon to new levels: the ability to highlight any passage, turn it into an image, and share it to social media. If the closest thing to immortality, for an author, is the ability for their output to be boiled down to a few easily disseminated sentences, the market will soon be brimming with prosaic vampires.

AIR QUOTES
When highlights make history.

RAWDAH MOHAMED

WORDS
MONA OMAR
PHOTO
LASSE FLØDE

Fashion's new gatekeeper invites everyone inside.

Rawdah Mohamed has no five-year plan. "I'm not goal-oriented," she says. "I don't even know what I'm doing next year." But that's not to say that she doesn't have a vision. The strength of her convictions and a can-do attitude have seen the Somali-Norwegian switch career from healthcare professional, to model, to viral activist, to fashion editor of the recently launched *Vogue* Scandinavia. When we speak, Mohamed has just stepped off a carousel of fashion weeks in Copenhagen, Stockholm and Oslo, and is excited about what she sees as a new moment in the industry. "I have a lot in common with emerging designers," she says. "We're a new generation in fashion that's more outspoken and the driving force for change."

MONA OMAR: How have you found the transition to the title of *Vogue* fashion editor?

RAWDAH MOHAMED: Fashion has always been a strong part of my identity. When I was young, I used to sleep at my grandmother's house just to see my aunts dress up before they went clubbing. I would be very upset if my aunt's shoes didn't match her skirt! And even before I joined *Vogue*, I would look at runways and make my own reviews of what I thought looked good. I would read magazines from cover to cover. The only difference for me is now I have a team to discuss these things with. It's the first time *Vogue* is in Scandinavia, so everyone really relies on each other.

MO: Did you always think you'd work in fashion?

RM: No. My father once gave me a book that said, "Don't shop where they won't hire you." It stuck with me. When I was growing up, the magazines were all very white and homogeneous. I didn't think they deserved my talent. I didn't think they deserved our money or our time.

MO: What changed?

RM: When social media came. That's when I found like-minded people and saw that there were people of color out there who were in fashion. When I think of fashion, I think of the people that I meet and those that are making the changes. I'm not talking about the CEOs.

MO: Your own online presence is often very funny. How do you balance that with the pressures of being a public figure?

RM: People really rely on you when you have a platform. I get a lot of stories from people about family relations or other issues or struggles. Perhaps it's easier to tell it to a stranger than it is to your own family. So, when I'm doing my stories, I like to think that I'm talking to my friends. But I don't try to be relatable for all who follow me. Some people follow me for fashion, other people follow me for activism and some people follow me for the jokes that I make. All these are a part of me on different days.

MO: Tell me about your personal style.

RM: Since I grew up in Scandinavia, I do like the minimalism and straight lines, but I believe I'm a bit more colorful than the average Scandinavian. What I really like is the mixing of cultures. I love the Somali theater that I grew up watching. The way they dance and express themselves, it's over the top. When they are angry, they are extremely angry, and when they love they *love*—really! In Norway, everything is sort of turned down a lot. Even the way we speak, it's such a calm way of speaking. If you mix the calmness with the complete opposite—loud music, dance all the time, expressive food and clothing—that's me.

MO: What are you hoping to achieve in your new role?

RM: I'm a huge fan of having some sort of challenge in life. The easiest way to get rid of me is if you say "yes" to me. If you say "no" you will not get rid of me. I think that if you are going to change the world just a tiny bit, you have to go where it is needed, right? I come from a health background, I worked at hospitals and at daycares and my hijab was never a question. My sister works at a lab and it's the same there. But in fashion, they're so behind, and that's why this is where the work needs to be done.

—

As a teenager, Mohamed was refused work at a mall store because the manager worried her hijab would be off-putting to customers. She responded with a personal campaign: "I went all around my neighborhood, to every house, and told everyone to not shop at that place."

TRASH TALK
On wish-cycling and wishful thinking.

WORDS
ALLYSSIA ALLEYNE
PHOTO
VICKI KING

For as long as there have been government-sponsored recycling programs, there has been wish-cycling—if not the word itself, then the logistical nightmare it represents. Within the context of, say, throwing a potato chip bag into the recycling and trusting it will be properly processed (it won't be), the term, coined in 2015 by recycling executive Bill Keegan, speaks to ignorance on the part of the consumer and exasperation on the part of the industry over poor sorting habits, contamination and inadequate infrastructures.

Wish-cycling (also known as aspirational recycling) is increasingly evoked in conversations about the plight of thrift shops, which regularly find themselves inundated with poor-quality items that cannot be sold on. Much like the potato chip bag in the recycling container, these garments must be diverted and disposed of on the charity's dime.[1]

But where a hapless recycler can blame their behavior on ignorance or inattention, the closet-clearing shopper has more to answer for. In a 2009 study published in *Clothing and Textiles Research Journal*, researchers at the University of Missouri and the University of North Carolina found that, for the majority of participants, clothing donation "provided a means to avoid the threat of feeling guilty about their consumption behavior."

If the recycling bin represents finality and accountability, the thrift shop represents possibility and redemption. To donate a garment you've tired of is to hope that where you see flaws, another may find value—a team hoodie with a flaking logo could be embraced for its authentic signs of wear; an impulse buy could find its way to someone more open to last summer's trends. Throwing the same garment directly into the garbage is to admit that something in which you've invested money or emotion is ultimately, indisputably, trash.

That so many people find themselves in this quandary is unsurprising; modern consumers buy clothes than any previous generation and ditch them much more quickly. Mitigating the pressures of wish-cycling, then, would require us to think more critically about the life span of our clothes at the time of purchase, rather than at the moment of disposal. It may mean more clothing left on the rack, but certainly fewer headaches for the thrift shop volunteer sifting through a mountain of irredeemable castoffs in search of a few saleable items.

(1) Similar problems occur following humanitarian disasters. One study, led by José Holguín-Veras, an expert on humanitarian logistics, found that between 50 to 70% of goods delivered during emergencies should not have been sent. These are costly and time-consuming mistakes because the donations require sorting and shipping over long distances, often when the transport infrastructure is in crisis.

DREAM HOUSE
The rise of renderporn.

WORDS
GEORGE UPTON
PHOTO
ZACH PHAN

In March 2021, a virtual, three-dimensional model of a house sold for more than half a million dollars. That the house didn't exist—it was designed by Toronto-based artist Krista Kim with software more commonly used to create video games—did not stop the digital render of the Martian-looking, glass-walled villa from reaching the same price as actual brick-and-mortar real estate. In an article published in *The New Yorker* a few months later, Anna Wiener (interviewed on page 115) decoded what had become a defining trend of the digital age.[1]

"Renderporn," as these hyperrealistic architectural fantasies have come to be known, is the product of recent developments in three-dimensional modeling software. Neoclassical architects like Giovanni Battista Piranesi may have been creating fantasy worlds back in the 18th century, but unlike his celebrated *capriccios,* or the subversive "paper architecture" of dissident Soviet architects, renderporn is uncannily lifelike and expresses no philosophical or political ideal. Instead, these aspirational, softly lit scenes of tasteful, expressive minimalism seem to serve as escapist fantasies into alternative realities.

Often set in real locations and featuring vintage furniture pieces, renderporn evokes a world of affluence and luxury where there is no climate emergency or financial hardship. Yet although the render's particular aesthetic is defined as much by the limitations of the software (simple, curved and textured surfaces are easier to create and look more convincing) as by the designer's personal style, renderporn will surely play a role in shaping real-world architectural aesthetics in the years to come.

(1) Common characteristics that Wiener identifies in these images include an atmosphere of calm, an absence of people and seasonality, an abundance of water, soft colors and warm light, and, overall, a visual language of affluent restraint.

HELLA JONGERIUS

WORDS
NANA BIAMAH-OFOSU
PHOTOS
NICK BALLÓN

The industrial designer on style at every scale.

For over 30 years, Hella Jongerius has been combining traditional craft techniques with contemporary processes, looking to the past to seek out innovative ideas. With her design studio, Jongeriuslab, she has worked at every scale imaginable, from designing Vitra's tiny yet iconic Coat Dots to the cabin interiors of the airline KLM. She is also an influential color theorist and the author of *I Don't Have a Favourite Colour: Creating the Vitra Colour & Material Library*.

For Jongerius, who lives in Berlin, design is rooted in the sort of personal inquiry that is also relevant to urgent societal questions, tackling the economy, culture, manufacturing and the human condition. Her most recent exhibition, *Woven Cosmos* at Berlin's Gropius Bau, asked questions about design in an age in which we must rapidly rethink our production and material consumption.

NANA BIAMAH-OFOSU: How would you define your ethos as a designer given the breadth of your practice?

HELLA JONGERIUS: I became a designer because I wanted to instigate change from within and push boundaries established in industrial design. I would describe my methodology as encompassing the process of an artist [but] with a strong social and political agenda, challenging the use of materials and production systems. I have my own questions as a designer so I am not interested in industrial design as just a service; I want to change something in the world using industrial design as a resource.

NBO: How are these questions generated? I'm interested to know whether there were objects in your childhood that made you question the role of design in everyday life.

HJ: I was raised on a farm with very little design or art around me, but this was also in the 1970s when as children we spent our free time making things. Activities such as knitting, embroidery and pottery were my way into becoming interested in materials. When it came to deciding what to study, I knew I wanted to pursue a creative discipline, but I wasn't comfortable with the lack of boundaries that come with art practice. Studying industrial design offered a creative outlet with a rigorous process.

NBO: How did your early career at Droog, a studio famed for its conceptual work, influence your practice?

HJ: When I started studying, I was confronted with a discipline still very much following modernist traditions, prioritizing form and appearance over what objects communicated. Through my education and early career, I found mentors who challenged these traditions and offered a way of stepping out of established design silos. This was incredibly liberating. The notions of perfection and imperfection became very important to me and I was intrigued by how imperfections could describe individuality within an industrial process. My questions have evolved and they are now focused on moral issues, artistic approaches and questioning the transformative and healing power of tactility.

Photography: Courtesy of Maharam

NBO: I'd like to talk a bit about design as an art and a science. Your work seems to approach it as both things at once.

HJ: The boundaries between art and science in my work are fluid. The duality is important because it is about understanding the sensory experience of an object while having the material knowledge to produce the desired effect.

NBO: How do you approach color in your work?

HJ: Color for me is a material. It is related to context—the object, its materiality and texture, as well as source of light and time of day. My work at Vitra has centered around creating a common library for material and color by understanding how designers use it in a contextual way—looking at their archives, understanding their surroundings and influences.[1]

NBO: You have previously said that "A color only becomes a color because it has neighbors." Can you describe how you developed your *Colour Catchers* as a response to this?

HJ: The *Colour Catchers* are multifaceted objects that we shaped from paper and painted in intensely rich pigments. They can catch light at different angles and are very useful in studying how colors look and feel in various conditions. I have always found the industry standard flat-surfaced color swatches incredibly limited and ridiculous. You can't truly understand the depth of a particular color unless it is seen in different instances and with shadows.

NBO: Your work is marked by its engagement with new technologies, but also with age-old craft techniques. What do these ideas offer in your work?

HJ: Let's take an example: weaving. Weaving is a coded process; you only have zero [a warp thread] and one [a weft thread]. Essentially, it is a digital process rooted in a very slow craft. It is a technique that has evolved within the industrial space and is now very efficient. However, the element of craft has been sacrificed and as a designer I see weaving as a craft rather than purely a process—it is a cultural topic, embedded in our language. This drive towards efficiency is why I started making my own looms—to dive into a new, innovative way of looking at weaving and making it about creativity again. We did this first at the Lafayette Anticipations foundation in Paris where we installed a loom that rose between the multistory levels of the building and over three months produced a 3D woven shape. [My recent] exhibition, *Woven Cosmos* at Gropius Bau in Berlin, is asking similar questions and inviting the public to participate. My most immediate question now is: What is the future of weaving? How do we combine traditional weaving with innovative techniques and work towards making stronger but lighter materials which will have multiple uses, such as in industrial manufacturing and construction?

NBO: Have these ideas generated prototypes? How might they apply to architecture and construction?

HJ: I am not interested in quick solutions but rather in developing holistic approaches. The joy of working with cultural institutions is that you have the luxury of getting lost—working for a commercial client doesn't always give you that opportunity. It is interesting to see where this work leads and what new innovations it may bring; I'm very much enjoying that.

NBO: It's also interesting to see design and efficiency as ideas related to the cosmos, as the title of the exhibition suggests. How do we retain the human scale as we rapidly innovate toward more digital technologies?

HJ: It is important that we maintain the human scale in our ways of production. This is how we continue to develop circular economies that can support reuse. We should only design or produce what the earth can handle. We've ruined our planet but we can also design our way out. This is now a much more urgent premise for designers than it was 20 or 30 years ago. In essence, I see the loom as cosmic, connected to weaving a new texture for the world; we can change our fate by choosing what we spin in this opportune world. It is about the human scale and maintaining our traces of humanity within design.

(1) Jongerius' work as Vitra's director of colors and materials is part of a concerted effort to step off the design conveyor belt of constantly manufacturing new objects. As she told *Dezeen* in 2014, "Why make new stuff every year?... Vitra has great stuff. It needs me on another level, and that is what I find interesting."

WORDS
JENNA MAHALE
PHOTO
DANIEL DORSA

CHAIN OF FOOLS
When peer pressure goes viral.

At around four in the morning on May 1, 2017, I was sent a magic cat. It did not fly through my half-open window, but appeared on my phone screen as ASCII text art: "Send this to 10 friends and you will ace your finals" read the words below its wand, conjuring clouds of asterisks, cedillas and commas.

While the missive was obviously good-natured, perhaps even adorable, there was a touch of quiet malevolence in its implication. Would a refusal to reproduce the message result in academic failure? And what if the recipient of the text doesn't have the requisite number of friends upon whom to inflict the curse further?

Last year, the writer Kathryn Schulz likened the increased transmission of chain communication to a timely disease: "Like a virus," she wrote in *The New Yorker,* "its sole purpose is replication." But arguably the true aim of a chain letter is to inspire fear: fear that you have wrought evitable misfortune on yourself; that the ghost you've always suspected of haunting your home will materialize; that a magic cat may indeed pass you over in his blessing of exam season sufferers; that you are not as well-liked as you'd like to be.

Many users noted an uptick in content that could be considered cringe during the initial wave of coronavirus lockdowns, a time of massive uncertainty and isolation. More than ever before, anything that felt "social" thrived online: riddles and recipes and filmed fitness challenges, but also, notably, misinformation. According to forwarded WhatsApp messages, the army was about to be deployed; monarchs lay on their deathbeds; and China had orchestrated it all.[1]

It may be the lure of a sense of control that's behind the proliferation of chain letters—that we could change the trajectory of our lives, or the world, by wielding the broadsword of instant communication. If we have power over anything, it is how loudly our digital avatars scream into the void.

(1) In 2020, WhatsApp set a new limit on frequently forwarded messages to curtail the volume of misinformation circulated through its interface. Any message that has already been forwarded more than five times is now flagged as such and cannot be sent on to more than one chat at a time.

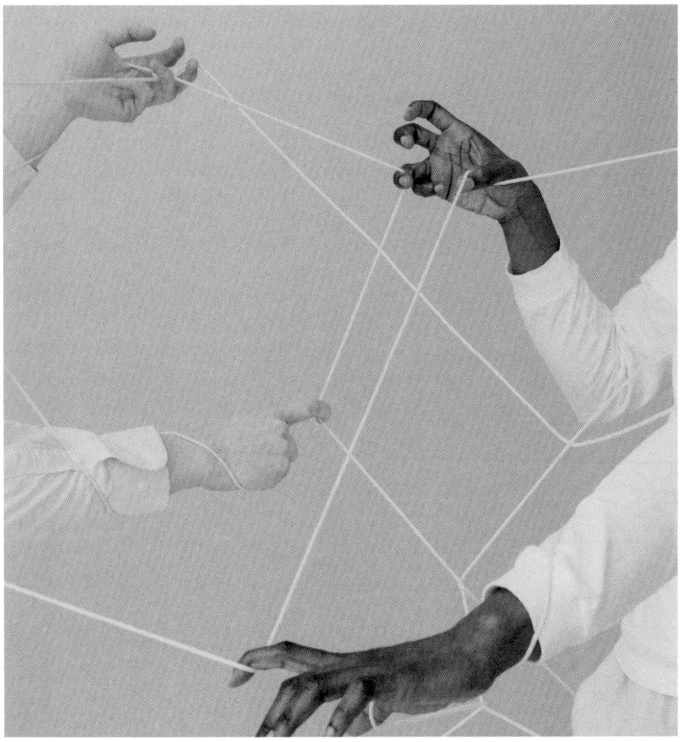

WORDS
OKECHUKWU NZELU
PHOTO
CECILIE JEGSEN

OUT OF OFFICE

The art of the auto-response.

Whether the cause is months of mounting pressure, a Sisyphean inbox or the insult of meetings insistently scheduled before 10 a.m., there's nothing more tantalizing than the thought of escaping work for a week, in my case to a cottage with no Wi-Fi.

Cue the out-of-office email. In theory, its premise is to let colleagues and correspondents know when you'll be back and who to contact with urgent queries in the meantime. In practice, however, the etiquette surrounding out-of-office responses varies—often to quite wild and, worse, wacky extremes. It is telling that some employers require a simple "I'll reply in a week," while others seemingly expect the precise geolocation of where you can be found if clients can't wait until tomorrow.

There are national cultures surrounding work and, subsequently, time away from it: Somewhere on the internet, a meme contrasting the archetypal European refusal to read emails during a vacation with the American equivalent is doing the rounds. "I am in the hospital. Email responses may be delayed by up to 30 minutes. Sorry for the inconvenience! If urgent, please reach me in the ER at..." reads the American example.

Stereotypes aside, European concepts of paid vacation are somewhat alien in the US: While the average EU worker receives 20 days paid leave every year, the average American worker gets just half as much. France even has the "right to disconnect"—the legal right to be cut off from emails when not working—an idea that has become all the more important in an age when technology makes connectivity inescapable (and the excuse of "intermittent access to emails" laughable).

Studies have long shown that real vacation time matters. In 2000, the University of Vienna found that people with proper vacation time experienced better sleep and moods. And, beyond the science, we have to ask ourselves what we're doing if we require employees to check emails while on sanctioned paid leave or to set out-of-office replies for an afternoon off. This culture of work suggests that our employers, by paying our bills, have bought not just our work but our lives.

Perhaps then, we'd be better off accepting that hard work is vital, but that hard work works best when kept in its place: Mondays to Fridays, 9 to 5, 49 weeks a year, not including federal holidays.

SIDE EFFECT
The Instragram filter as art form.

When Instagram made its augmented reality software available to the public in August 2019, the platform was quickly flooded with novel, user-generated effects that alter your appearance and surroundings. Suddenly, it seemed, anyone with the time and inclination could create a filter that made it appear as if you were wearing comically large glasses or had sprouted dog's ears. But the technology quickly caught the attention of contemporary artists too.

Filters were developed to be a fun way to engage with followers, but many artists have been drawn by the ability to play with a sense of self and subvert the pressures to conform on social media. In the surreal Dream Machine effect by Mitsuko Ono, for example, a carousel of colorful figures, all wearing your face, spins slowly around your head. Adrian Steckeweh's effects erase the self entirely, creating the impression that your face is melting or dissolving in a cascade of pixels.

A filter on Instagram offers artists certain advantages over traditional, gallery-based artwork. Not only can they engage directly with the viewer, making them part of the work, but there is no limit to the number of people who can participate. So uploading a filter to one of the most popular mobile applications can allow artists a far greater reach than any physical gallery space.

Though the technology is still developing, AR filters have the potential to radically impact the art world, changing how we engage with—and what we consider to be—art, while allowing artists themselves to circumvent the gallery system. For now, though, whether you're experiencing momentary ego death or seeing what you look like with Steve Buscemi's eyes, filters remain a particularly fun way to pass the time.

—

WORDS
GEORGE UPTON

Left Photo: Bea De Giacomo, Right Photo: Laurence Leenaert / LRNCE

PILLOW TALK

WORDS
NATHAN MA
PHOTO
JOE HORNER

A lucid conversation about dream logic.

In *The Committee of Sleep,* published in 2001, Dr. Deirdre Barrett examines strokes of genius and the dreams that inspired them. Reviewing the work of Beethoven, Dalí, Paul McCartney and biologist Margie Profet, the Harvard Medical School professor posits that we possess the power to solve our waking lives' problems while fast asleep.

In the 20 years since the book was first published, the way we sleep has drastically changed: We work too much and stay up too late, and personal electronics can interrupt the rest we do get. Amid a global pandemic, Barrett still believes the answers we seek are closer than we might imagine—if only we're willing to dream.

NATHAN MA: Are dreams wiser than waking thoughts?

DEIRDRE BARRETT: It would be really remarkable if they were. We don't remember the majority of our dream content, so it would be terribly cruel and also just nonsensical, in a Darwinian sense, for this piece of our experience that we remember ephemerally to be better advice than our waking logic. Waking thought has very clearly evolved to be maximally advantageous to survival, while sleep is mainly doing restorative processes in our body. A lot of the characteristics of dreaming have to do with which brain areas are shut down because the neurotransmitters are being replenished.

NM: Is the thinking we do in dreams qualitatively different?

DB: We dream about all of our usual thoughts, concerns, hopes and fears, but we're just in a very different state of consciousness: more emotional, less logical, less linear and with more visual imagery. Our dreams seem more obvious if we think about the analogous thoughts we have while awake.

NM: Last year, you published *Pandemic Dreams*—a global survey of how our dreams were shifting in parallel with the pandemic. What did you discover?

DB: Swarms of bugs, entering solitary confinement or coming down with the virus—the dreams that were common early on in the pandemic show up wherever lockdowns are still happening. But interpretations can change. I saw a few dreams where the pandemic was over and the dreamer was back in their favorite crowded setting, like a nightclub or a sporting event. Early on, people always commented that they woke up and felt a huge wave of sadness and an immense sense of loss, like they were being tormented with images of the past. But more recently, people began to say that they felt cheered up—they associated it with the future. It can read like the same dream, but the effect is reversed.

NM: How can dreams help us process experiences of grief and loss more generally?

DB: I did a study on dreams about grief, and they tend to evolve over time. In the first few days or weeks, dreams tend to be negative, directly reenacting the loss and the death. And then people begin to have more positive dreams related to death: the kinds where you get to say what you wished you had said, and bid someone goodbye in a way that feels satisfying. In these dreams, you get closure, or they give you gifts that symbolized that they were incorporating as a part of you. Further down the road, dreams about those who died would include the person coming back to give advice, as if you were carrying this person who had your best interests at heart. People describe these dreams as profoundly comforting, but they seem equally comforted by the idea that they had psychologically incorporated the person. These dreams weren't really about the fact that the person was dead, but the fact that you'd ever known them.

—

—

Barrett recently collaborated with Coors on a project to see if certain stimuli could compel people to dream of beer. The study prompted an open letter from other scientists to the FTC arguing that "Our dreams cannot become just another playground for corporate advertisers."

THE LANGUAGE OF HOME
How weird words forge new friendships.

WORDS
OKECHUKWU NZELU
PHOTO
OGHALÉ ALEX

You might not have heard the word "familect" before, but chances are you're already fluent in it. Does your family have an unusual word for the remote control that outsiders wouldn't recognize? Do you have a nickname that everyone at the office calls you? Does your friendship group have a catchphrase that's followed you through the years?

Familect—the idiosyncratic use of language that is particular to a distinct social group, not necessarily a family—is a common linguistic phenomenon. When individuals spend a lot of time together, the language they use changes: Words born from a particular joke or incident slip into common parlance; the rules of grammar and pronunciation are bent and broken; we speak, effectively, in a kind of code. Years ago, an Italian friend and I stayed in a Milan apartment which was advertised as "well collegated": In a funny quirk of language, the owner had used a mix of "well-connected" and its Italian equivalent, "*ben collegato.*" Since then, whenever either of us moves home or stays in a hotel on vacation, we ask each other the all-important question: "But is it well collegated?"

Famous people are no exception. In an episode of Netflix's *The Crown*, the royal family refers to Buckingham Palace as "the house," in what is presumably an ironic use of profound understatement. (The episode also shows a young Diana, during her engagement to Prince Charles, not realizing what this term means—and Camilla Parker Bowles somewhat pointedly disabusing her.)

Familect is universal, and yet *how* we use it is part of what makes each family or social circle unique. Research shows that familect is an important part of how we celebrate intimacy with loved ones. In 1981, a team led by communications expert Robert Hopper found that what we now refer to as familect is part of a broader system of language which also includes sharing our thoughts, feelings, and other things which we may keep secret, and using certain "emotion-laden nonverbal channels," such as body language that might not be appreciated or understood in a more public context. As *The Crown's* example shows, there can be an exclusive dimension to all of this: Like any code, it partly functions to separate insiders, who are familiar and beloved, from outsiders, who are not.

While there is an exclusivity to familects, they are also an example of how language can be democratized—that the rules we usually observe without thinking are established by people just like us.[1] What seems rigid becomes fluid and pliable; what seems stern and ungiving becomes a plaything in our hands. And, more than this, familect crystallizes the fact that joyful experimentation with language is not just our right but an unshakable habit—without it, many of our intimate relationships would sound quite different, and probably look quite different too. Both universal and private, familect captures our feelings of closeness to one another—of being "well collegated," if you will—and our most precious moments of expressive playfulness, and preserves them perfectly for the times when we might need to be reminded that life can, in fact, be fun.

(1) Slang is easy to establish within a family because the user group is cohesive and small. Slang words that exist among larger groups, for example, teenagers, are often popularized via songs or TV shows rather than individuals (as *Mean Girls'* Gretchen Wieners learned the hard way when she tried to make "fetch" happen).

AUDIENCE PARTICIPATION

The new rules for watching movies.

Photo: Sylvia Ballhause

In the US and many other countries, you may only ever be reminded that you're sharing a darkened movie theater with hundreds of other people when a ripple of laughter or the occasional gasp erupts; in India, however, the cinema is a collective and interactive experience. Viewers will cheer and sing along, shouting to the characters or throwing coins at the screen in celebration. If the movie is met with disapproval, the crowd will not suffer in silence.

With a slew of new interactive features recently launching on streaming services, we might all soon enjoy a more participatory experience of the movies: Netflix has Netflix Party, Amazon Prime includes Amazon Watch Party and Disney Plus offers GroupWatch. These "virtual parties," designed to allow viewers to watch along with remote friends and family, were developed in response to how we're all spending more time at home. But they may ultimately come to change the way we engage with the big screen.

As Lakshmi Srinivas observes in her book, *House Full: Indian Cinema and the Active Audience,* such lively audience interaction not only enhances the viewing experience, but also provides valuable feedback for filmmakers. With more active participation piloted at home, could we see a noisier return to theaters the world over?

WORDS
GEORGE UPTON

WORDS
RYAN WILLMS
PHOTO
JUSTIN CHUNG

Saehee Cho on cooking as a catalyst for community.

Saehee Cho is a cook, food stylist and writer based in Los Angeles who, during the COVID-19 pandemic, also became an impromptu greengrocer. When the lockdown tightened its grip on California, local farms began to feel the pinch of restaurant closures, disrupted supply chains and canceled farmers markets. In response, Cho leaned on relationships she had cultivated during her 12 years in the catering business and launched Soon Mini—a food subscription service connecting farmers directly to consumers. As part of our *Slow Systems* series with Samsung, Cho describes how the opportunity also presented her with the chance to do what she loves most: create—and care for—a community through food.

RYAN WILLMS: What's your approach in the kitchen?

SAEHEE CHO: There are two types of cooking for me. There's the "work cooking" which is catering—doing scale, styling, that stuff—and then there's the kind of cooking I do for my friends. If I have a catering job, I'm maybe not sleeping for two nights, and my body feels pretty thrashed by the end of it. I don't even want to look at food. But when I have friends coming over for a dinner party, and we're all just going to make some hand rolls or cut up some fruit, I already know it's going to be great because it's with people I love. I'm very intentional about thinking about them as I cook. Loving other people through food is essentially what I call "mom cooking."

RW: Is "mom cooking" how you would describe your repertoire?

SC: My food is not the fanciest; it's not tweezer perfect. There's an abundance to it, and that bounty can be messy sometimes, but I love that. Food, for me, has always been a domestic realm. Once you start to commodify food, it becomes a sport, and the restaurant world has been deliberate about cutting women out of it. I've always been a femme person, and I'm not ashamed of that. I cook in a more feminine way, and to me, that means it's intimate, it means smaller and it means using food that's more satisfying to cook with and serve. It also makes a more memorable meal.

RW: How has that sense of community carried over from your cooking into Soon Mini?

SC: In March 2020, at the beginning of the lockdown, I started delivering meals to some close friends who had just had babies and were definitely not going to grocery stores. I realized that people didn't actually need prepared meals—they had an excess of time to cook for themselves. What they needed were ingredients that they could trust and food that they felt good about. I'd been working in catering for 12 years, so I had relationships with some small farms and a working knowledge of seasonality in produce. I was able to get wholesale prices for large bulk orders, and it was a great way to say "hi" to my friends from a distance—I would see them through the window, and there was just this really sweet and genuine interaction. I realized that all supply chains can be simple.

RW: What else have you learned through your new venture?

SC: My relationship with nature has changed. Because I understand it takes nine months to grow cabbage, I'm not going to waste that cabbage. I don't know why it isn't part of the basic curriculum to just watch a seedling grow. You can't speed up nature. Well, you *can*, but there are consequences. It's important to understand that the world has a rhythm already prescribed to it.

RW: How have you been taking care of your own daily rhythm?

SC: When you live in a city, you think you can be stronger than your body, that you can tolerate more than you can. But there's a cost for when you just give, give, give. You have to take back too; like that cabbage, you need to be replenished. What I try to do, at the very least, is to portion out time for the things that I love: food and writing.

Left: Smart Bespoke 4-Door Flex™ Refrigerator by Samsung

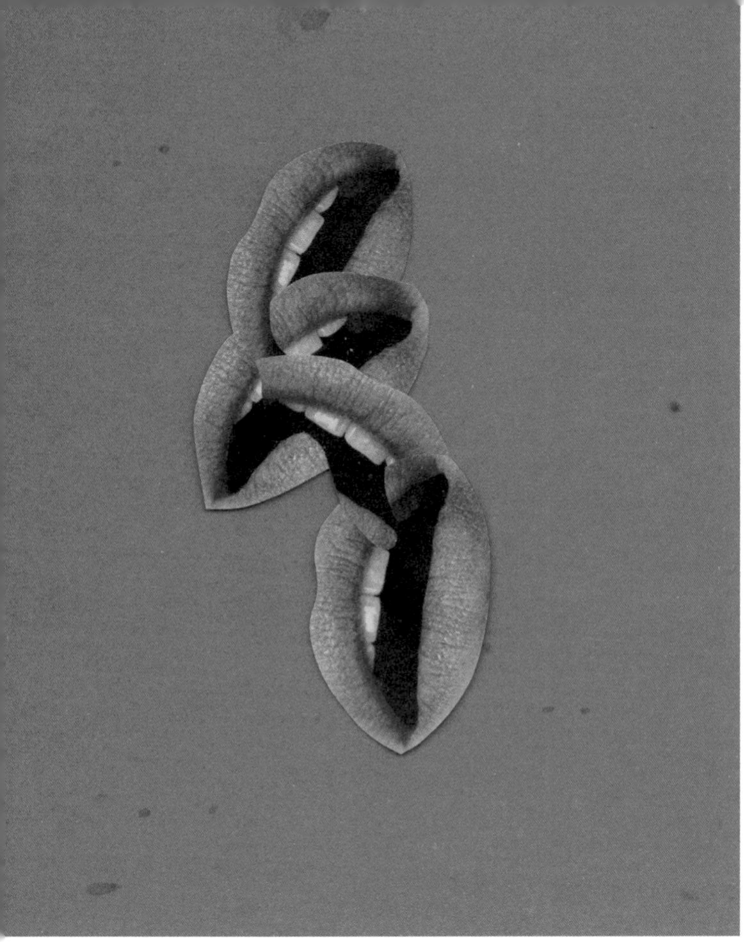

PAUSE FOR THOUGHT
Why filler words are like, um, good.

There are things the world doesn't need. The banana slicer, for example, when a knife gets the job done just fine, or shoes for babies. For generations of linguists, filler words have fallen into the same category. The common belief is that they add little to a dialogue aside from making the speaker sound nervous ("uh"), juvenile ("like") or insecure ("sort of"). Yet, verbal fillers are a major part of how we talk, featuring in virtually every spoken sentence. Humanity tends to bend toward efficiency, so why would we collectively persist in wasting our breath on "ums" and "ahs"?

A recent strain of research has sought to prove that filler words can help hold a conversation. In 2017, dozens of language experts from this new school of thought challenged *The New York Times* for publishing an article telling readers to stop using "not so smart" filler words. Among them was linguistic anthropologist Dr. Jena Barchas-Lichtenstein, who, in response to the piece, wrote in *Quartz* about "the many valuable functions these words play." She argues that "we can't be socially appropriate beings without them" as they "add nuance and richness to our speech," making us more considerate speakers and listeners alike.

Not only do filler words warn the listener that the other person is getting their thoughts together and that therefore they should not interrupt, but they also give the speaker a toolbox of linguistic devices for expressing their emotional stance in a polite, thoughtful and more considered manner. You don't need to be a linguist to realize that the simple addition of a "kind of" can soften criticism ("it's kind of bad") or that a "like" can make an exaggerated statement sound more trustworthy ("I had, like, a million things to do").

Filler words are far more than filler; when used strategically and in moderation, they help us communicate more effectively and feel better connected to the person we're speaking to. We aren't robots after all. It's okay to sound, um, a little human.

WORDS
ANNICK WEBER
PHOTO
ROZENN LE GALL

BOX FRESH
The odd appeal of unboxings.

WORDS
SALOME WAGAINE
PHOTO
TINE BEK

The thrill of unboxing predates the social media trend for watching videos of it. Opening up a box containing new, uniform-compliant school shoes can be as exciting for a child as unwrapping a birthday present. Despite their future being clear—several seasons' worth of scuffing before they start to pinch—for a moment those shoes are spick-and-span, perfectly arranged and full of promise.

Recently, this thrill has taken an odd twist: There are currently more than 100,000,000 videos on YouTube featuring people opening products and packages. The first video described as an "unboxing" (item: a Nokia cell phone) was uploaded in 2006. Since then, these videos have come to serve as reviews, relaxation aids and a glimpse of a life less budget-strapped—sometimes all at once. Content ranges from people opening up the latest phone or multimedia release, to luxury fashion and beauty items, to the more bespoke. In the summer of 2018, US gymnast Shawn Johnson appeared on a series of videos: "UNBOXING MY OLYMPIC SILVER MEDALS!" and, the sequel, "UNBOXING my Olympic GOLD medal." The titles are urgent, blandly descriptive and unabashedly enticing.

Many companies understand that telegenic packaging increases the likelihood that their product will be plugged by influencers receiving PR gifts: holographic paper perfect for a Boomeranging mini-clip on Instagram stories, for example, and boxes with one long flap to cover the top rather than four shorter ones, making it easier to open them one-handed while holding a camera.

Watching someone show off their wares on-screen is a way of satiating a curiosity—perhaps even nosiness—about the lives of those wealthier or more fortunate. These videos give you the skinny on what it's really like to get a designer handbag, for instance. You learn about where the additional strap goes, how big the interior compartments are, and also how it will be presented to you: Expect a canvas dustcover to protect your latest splurge. While the videos cannot induct you into an exclusive club, they familiarize you with its rules. We have always been fascinated by the rich and famous; unboxing takes us one step closer to imagining what that life might feel like.

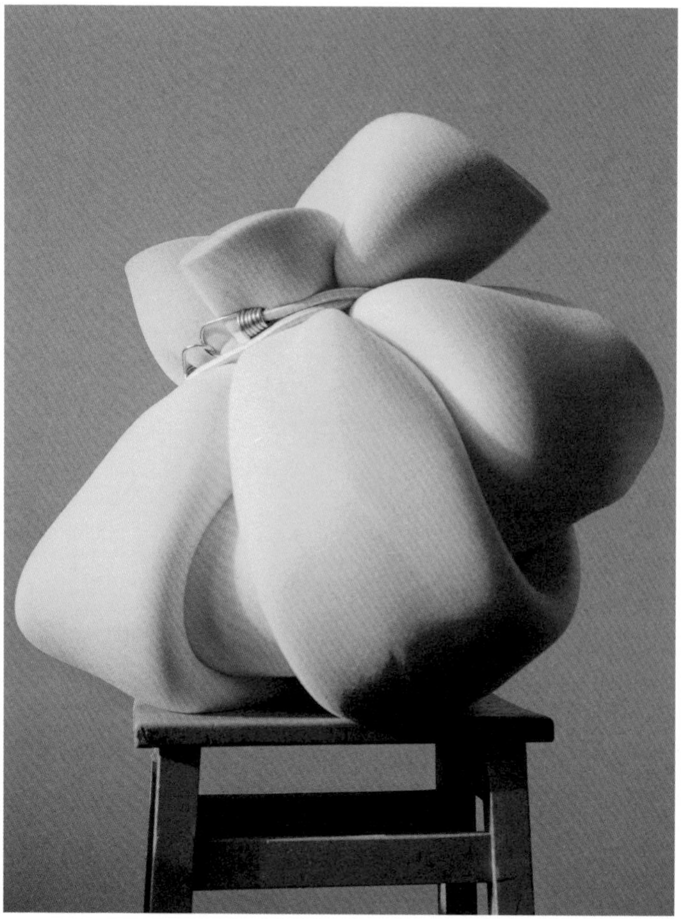

WORD: HYPEROBJECT

A word for things too huge to name.

Etymology: The term "hyperobject" was coined by environmental philosopher Timothy Morton in 2008 with the goal of gifting humans a word to describe things that are within our understanding but beyond our immediate grasp. Because we tend to think of objects as items we can fit within our field of vision, Morton added the prefix "hyper," which means "over" or "beyond" in Greek, suggesting excess or exaggeration. We can conceptualize hyperobjects, but we cannot see them as a whole.

Meaning: Some things are so vast that we will never witness them fully: global warming, black holes, all the Styrofoam cups in the world, ever. You don't know their exact number, but you know that number is finite and that they're everywhere. You may have googled how long it takes for Styrofoam to decompose (500 years). Perhaps you already suspected it, but now you know for sure: Those flimsy cups will outlive you by centuries. Your coffee-to-go is now tied to this enormous, scary thought. Congratulations, you just encountered a hyperobject.

All hyperobjects share common traits, according to Morton: They are "viscous," meaning they won't go away; they're "nonlocal," meaning they exist and expand on a global scale; finally, they're "inter-objective," meaning they are made of many different things, but cannot be reduced to one of these things alone. The sum of all Styrofoam cups in the world isn't the same as the sum of all parts of each individual cup.

Morton says that understanding hyperobjects forces an "upgrade" in the human brain. Our ability to conceptualize something greater than ourselves and to anticipate consequences that will outlast our time on Earth means it's more likely we will feel compelled to act, they argue. If we can comprehend global warming despite not being able to take in all the ways in which it will manifest itself, we cannot reasonably decide to look away. Our newfound awareness helps us rewire our brains to tackle new challenges. Morton likens it to seeing someone about to get hit by a car: Because we know they're about to be hurt or killed, we must try to save them. By design, hyperobjects make us hypersensitive to some of the biggest crises of our time.

Artwork: Tara Donovan. Photo: Ruth Clark. Courtesy of Jupiter Artland

WORDS
DAPHNÉE DENIS

WORDS
RACHEL CONNOLLY
PHOTO
OLIVER MAYHALL

Obvious self-promotion feels tawdry. This is especially true in the age of social media, when constantly marketing ourselves (to whom, exactly?) has become so easy, addictive and sophisticated.

This is what makes the concept of a public intellectual contradictory. Too many TV and radio appearances; the churning pressure of a weekly column (bound to consist, partly, of mundane meditations); tweeting too much or in a way that tries too hard to be funny; going on a comedy quiz show. All of these things risk denigrating the standing of an intellectual and transforming them, in the public imagination, into the sort of person whose career has "pop" as its prefix. It's a delicate balance to strike.

There has been a lot written about the decline of the public intellectual. But these pieces often operate from a false premise, comparing the standing of, say, an esteemed academic philosopher at Oxford in our era, to the reputation of John Berger in the 1960s. So, how can a specialist become well-known to the general public without seeming unserious?

The issue is not that a fidgety public has suddenly started ignoring a type of figure they used to revere, but that academic philosophy is not as resonant to contemporary concerns as Berger's work was at the time. Berger was not an academic, however, but a figure whose work became popular for rigorously addressing the aesthetic and technological concerns of his era.

When I consider what a truly modern public intellectual might look like, I think not of historians or philosophers but of the internet. And then of a man named Evgeny Morozov, whose work blogging about the social implications of technology and surveillance led to him earning a PhD from Harvard, and to write regularly for places like *The Guardian* and *The New York Times* about privacy, data collection and Silicon Valley in a funny, engaging way.

Self-promotion works best when it is subtle and serendipitous; when your audience feels almost as if they have stumbled upon someone who was not seeking to be discovered.

AN OPEN MIND
The making of a modern public intellectual.

50 — 112

D

EV

Words
KYLA MARSHELL

Photography
KATIE MCCURDY

THE BOUNDLESS POTENTIAL

OF BEING A MASTER OF NONE.

Over the last several years, the musical artist known as Dev Hynes has blossomed into a Renaissance artist known for so much more. After releasing music in the band Test Icicles in his native UK, he moved to the US in 2007 and performed as Lightspeed Champion, before debuting as Blood Orange in 2011.[1] Under this, his best-known moniker, he has produced records that mix electronica and R & B, laced with his own tender, melancholic falsetto. In addition to five Blood Orange albums, he's become a scorer for film and TV (HBO's series *In Treatment* and the 2019 movie *Queen & Slim*, among them), and collaborated with artists one rarely gets to hear strung together in one sentence: Philip Glass, Toro y Moi, Solange, Project Pat, Diddy.

Along with his own records have come a series of beautifully shot music videos—poetic, whimsical and off-center without being self-conscious. Which is how their director—yes, it's Dev, again—comes across when speaking about his artistic output. Doing it all—from making the music to designing the albums' typeface—isn't born out of a maniacal need for control, but rather a question and a challenge: *What can I do?*

KM: You've worked under a number of different names—Blood Orange, Lightspeed Champion, and your own name for scoring work. Where do those alter egos come from, if that's what they are, and what purpose do they serve?

DH: I've always felt like there's so many sides to every person—so many different moods and interests, even within a day. We fluctuate so much. In my experience in music, especially if you're not a white male, you're not really allowed to have different moods. So, intentionally-slash-subconsciously, I liked the idea of differentiating between everything just so that when I do something [new], afterwards people aren't like, "Well, he's doing something different!"

KM: When you're collaborating on a song with another artist, or you're doing a score for film or TV, how do you take on the essence of that other presence while also bringing your own vision to it?

DH: I've known a few people that have wanted to get into scoring, but one thing that they don't understand is that beyond it being extremely collaborative, you're also at-service. That's something that can be tough for some people because you put a lot of work into it, and then someone who is not musical will just be like, "Do it again." It's kind of an interesting part of my brain because I'm putting emotion into it, usually because I'm relating to the story, but I'm also not fully precious with it. It can be very technical sometimes. Almost like solving a puzzle. I mean, I don't do puzzles—but I imagine that when people do puzzles they feel a sense of completion! And it's not necessarily they feel a *creative* sense of completion, but they feel something nonetheless. That's kind of what scoring is like.

(1) Test Icicles was a rough and ready punk trio. Despite only releasing one record, the band was popular on the UK gig circuit. As Hynes told music magazine *NME* when they split: "We were never, ever that keen on the music. I understand that people liked it, but we personally, er, didn't."

KM: What is it that allows you not to be precious about it?

DH: Thirty to 40% of songs that I've written or been a part of have then become other people's. Stuff I'm working on that would probably end up being Blood Orange stuff, and they've just heard it and liked it and had an idea. I'm never working on something and in my mind I'm like, "This is going to be on my album." I always want outside minds to interact with things, because then it takes it somewhere that's outside of my head. If I trust and respect someone then I'm not really that precious. I just think there's really great strength in knowing what you can do and what you can bring. And also knowing what you can't do.

KM: Some artists, even if they want to explore different disciplines or genres or instruments, don't feel like they're "allowed" to. How did you come to be so varied in your creativity?

DH: I was talking with a friend recently about how there's different types of creativity. There's some people who maybe think of the title of being an artist first, and then work to get there. Then other people are just taking stuff in and learning, and what's spun out of that becomes something creative. And I think I'm that type. Blood Orange is a form of expression. If it was to be simplified to one goal, the goal is just to see what I can do. I'm using music as a route and then exploring all of these things that I see and feel inspired by, to see if I can make anything that's even slightly close to any of those worlds that I'm a really big fan of.

> "There's really great strength in knowing what you can do and also what you can't do."

KM: What kind of music were you interested in as a kid?

DH: I was playing classical when I was growing up, but a really big thing beyond that is music videos and MTV. In England, we had some really random music video channels. It's how I learned a lot. Being in Essex, there weren't many avenues to explore in music. It was either going to the library to rent out CDs, stealing CDs from Virgin Megastores or watching MTV.[2] In a day, they could play Alice in Chains, into Destiny's Child, into Slipknot, into LL Cool J, into the Pet Shop Boys—that's kind of how my brain works. All of those things were so inspiring for me, so I've just run with it.

KM: What do you think about the concept of mastery? Is it something you value?

DH: Instrument-wise, I'm not a master at anything. But something I think I'm pretty good at is starting and finishing. I think it's a real

(2) Many of Hynes' music videos draw on naturalistic imagery of life in New York. However, for "Benzo" (2019), he appears in a highly stylized, Marie Antoinette-esque world. Speaking to *Vogue*, he explained that he aimed to push his boundaries. "I wanted to try to make one of those videos where this world exists only within this music video."

Groomer: Dana Boyer, Photo Assistant: Alec Lesser

Reebok

strength that I got to a point where I was able to really understand that, because it opened up a whole world of people. To me, there's nothing better than a room full of people who all know exactly what they're good at. And that's kind of the Blood Orange energy, anyway. It's really an idea that's been started and finished by me. And then the middle can just be a free-for-all.

KM: What kind of things did you do to soothe or comfort yourself during quarantine?

DH: Reading a lot. I mean, more than usual reading. Like a crazy amount. And going deeper into sports, which is really my first love in the world.

KM: Do you play any sports?

DH: I'm a psycho tennis fan. I play every day of my life. And I play football—as in, soccer. I was playing on two teams. I recently had to stop because of an injury, but at the end of the season I'm going to come back. Tennis and football have just been my entire life, really. That was the beginning of my life and so it's come back with a vengeance. I think we sometimes believe we can't really do things when we're older, or pick things back up, because we think it's a negative that we can't master it. And that holds a lot of people back from doing the things that are very enjoyable, very fun and educational. There is this idea that if you can't do something really, really well then maybe you shouldn't do it. And I'm strongly against that.

This may sound kind of crazy, but I feel like all the Blood Orange shit is really that. Everything to do with it is for fun, and to just appease myself. I mean, for example, I didn't study graphic design, but I've done all the artwork. If there's a tour poster, I've done every single one, and merch, and all that kind of stuff. I don't want to be a master of graphic design.[3] It's not something I want to explore and I have zero interest in doing it for other people. But it's a fun thing for me to play around with, within the context of this world that I've been lucky to be able to create and work in.

KM: At this stage in your life, what has been the most surprising development or revelation?

DH: Lately, I feel like I care even less about outside noise. Even though I cared little before. And that's in terms of—it sounds so cliché—social media, Instagram, and all that kind of stuff. I almost have a determination, in regard to real-world experiences.[4]

KM: You mean a determination to have real-world experiences?

DH: Yeah, but not in the sense of like, traveling to Egypt, but more like in the sense of talking to people. Because people are trying to convince us that everything lives inside this tiny phone, and I just feel like it's really dark. It really grosses me out. And I just want nothing to do with it. I want to have my family, my friends and my loved ones, and I just want to exist in the world.

KM: Have you considered directing a feature-length film?

(3) Over two days in June 2020, Hynes raised over half a million dollars for the Movement For Black Lives and the LGBTQ Freedom Fund by selling a T-shirt designed with the brand Brain Dead. The text on the T-shirt read "If You Love Black Culture Protect Black Lives," which he intended as a critique of non-Black artists who mined the culture without stepping into the Black Lives Matter protests.

DH: I've thought about it. When people do a lot of different things, I think it's still always good to respect the art form. I never just want to jump into it. I want it to feel as natural for me as when I do Blood Orange stuff. I don't necessarily know how that can happen but I want to get to a point where it becomes a very natural form of expression.

KM: What's next for Blood Orange, in terms of what you're creating and what you hope to create?

DH: Unsure. In between every Blood Orange project I never really know if there's another one, if I'm honest. I'm always aware there would be, but I have no idea when or how. I'm working on stuff because I'm always working on stuff. There's definitely no live shows, for a fact. That's something I can guarantee. No live shows about to happen in any form for a long time. But maybe music in two years.

(4) Hynes first quit social media in 2015, writing on Facebook of the disconnect he felt between his online presence and lived experiences. "You may see me write on this page or playing music and see me as Blood Orange or Dev Hynes, but I turn the corner and I am just another black man," he wrote.

A luminous celebration of gelatin.

61 LIGHT SNACK

Photography & Styling DOAN LY

(bio) Doan Ly, who both created and photographed these gelled objects, is the founder of a.p. bio—a creative studio in New York usually focused on floral design.

Q&A:
DOAN LY
Words by Harriet Fitch Little

HFL: What's it like, working with gelatin?

DL: Incredibly fun. We literally clap when we release a new shape from the molds. We use mainly found shapes from objects around the studio so it's really fun to see what impression a vase or a cup makes in jelly form. It's like the secret life of objects. Once you start, you can't stop your mind from trying to find other forms. It's pure, childlike glee and completely disproportionate pride.

HFL: Why is it such an appealing medium to photograph?

DL: I love color. Here, I get to mix them and the palette is always so joyful, even if the colors are dark. You can't take gelatin seriously, even when it tries to be moody. It jiggles! It's also fun to shoot because it reflects light, it's shiny, it's partly translucent. And though it's a still-life, the shapes take on a bend because of the nature of the material.

HFL: Your floral still-life images have influenced current aesthetics in the genre. Are you tempted to tackle food photography next?

DL: Oh wow—you must have heard this from my mom! I love shooting food, though I don't get much of a chance to do so. I don't get as much access to photogenic food as I do to flowers. Food, feasting, fruit and other aspects of gathering are very much key characters in still-life composition. I just wish I had more time and resources to experiment.

Not your therapist, not your friend: What accounts for the remarkable rise of the life coach?

ESSAY: THE GOAL KEEPERS

Words
LAVENDER AU

In certain circles, life coaches are seemingly everywhere. Over the past year, for example, I have heard about their merits from sources including a New York gallery owner and a Filipino businessman in the shipping industry. Then, at a dinner party in Düsseldorf last month, I was seated across from a coach who coached other coaches to lead seminars.

I was skeptical about this multibillion-dollar industry and the language of positivity that surrounds and fuels it.[1] Critics of the self-improvement industry as a whole see it as born from the woes of late capitalism: With social mobility so out of reach, self-improvement creates a facade of progress. Obsessing about the self is easier than reforming society.

But this truth, which is structural, doesn't necessarily mean that there isn't value to be found in life coaching on a personal level—if you can afford it. The gallery owner credited her coach with helping her feel lighter and happier, and being a better leader. She says she became more accountable to herself and those around her, and had a greater sense of self-worth. Life coaches say that their clients—or "players," as some prefer to call them—are not coming to them to be cured. They simply need some help in the game of life. They seek change, to become their best possible selves.

So I book myself in for a free taster session with Charlene Birk, the gallery owner's coach. We meet on Zoom, since Birk is based in Florida and I'm in Germany at the time of our call. Her Zoom background—a spacious office lobby with potted plants—was chosen, she explains, for its "calm, focus and simplicity."

Birk begins by telling me that coaching is not giving advice, since "clients have the answers." When I tell her about things I want to do, she gives positive reinforcement: "That's absolutely within your reach!" When I talk about what I consider to be my achievements, she exclaims, "Congratulations!" There is none of the emotional payback or reciprocal listening you might have to do for a friend. Within my session, I hear nothing about Birk's own life experiences.

Many life coaches work directly with companies to coach high-value employees; although life coaching is a holistic industry, success at work features heavily within it. If you're paying for it yourself, the services of a coach would cost somewhere between $275 and $1,500 a month, which might include three to four sessions and email follow-ups. A certain level of material privilege is needed to afford this service, which leads to an obvious paradox: The client paying for a personal quest of self-discovery is already quite successful, at least in terms of income bracket.[2] Just as we're increasingly outsourcing physical labor to apps and their workers to get things like groceries, those who can afford it are now taking their thoughts to coaches, rather than to friends or family.

Though life coaching may seem like a new phenomenon—an offshoot of the Instagram-fueled idea that our whole lives should be inspiring—it has a long lineage. Beth Blum, author of *The Self-Help Compulsion: Searching for Advice in Modern Literature*, tells me, "There have been individuals eager to profit from people's desperation

> "Social media has democratized coaching, and led to its blurring with other forms of aspirational content."

(1) According to the International Coaching Federation (IFC), the estimated global total revenue from coaching in 2019 was $2.8 billion—a 21% increase since 2015.

(2) In 2019, *Condé Nast Traveler* reported that "extreme life coaching" had become a travel trend for the world's one-percenters: "Players" are dropped into the wilderness with a team of life coaches for up to six months, and spend $265,000 in the process.

for good advice long before modern capitalism came around." (Life coaches might disagree with her characterization, since, as Birk had explained to me, they don't give advice.)

"It's always been there," agrees Marion Goldman, author of *The American Soul Rush: Esalen and the Rise of Spiritual Privilege*. "People want their lives to be better. It's one of the reasons why they get involved in various mainstream religions."

Goldman says that life coaching has its roots in earlier forms of alternative guidance. From the 1930s onward, a number of spiritual and psychological disciplines set up shop in the United States. The Human Potential Movement (HPM), which took root in California in the 1960s, was particularly influential in the formation of life coaching as we know it. It disrupted the previously dominant understanding of the good life as one that involved holding down a stable job. A key tenet was that everyone could take the steps necessary to fulfill the extraordinary human potential that lay within them.[3]

" It's really a sort of Wild West.
You could call yourself a life coach."

The format of life coaching today is less explicitly spiritual than its forebears, however: It's self-improvement for a growing demographic that shies away from organized religion (although they might embrace practices like meditation). While the industry is not regulated, multiple credentialing bodies are vying to validate new coaches.[4] "It's really a sort of Wild West," says Goldman. "*You* could call yourself a life coach."

(3) The Institutes for the Achievement of Human Potential was an early precursor to the HPM; it was founded in 1955 on the principle that "every child born has, at the moment of birth, a greater potential intelligence than Leonardo da Vinci ever used."

(4) According to a 2020 study by the IFC, 74% of coach practitioners said they currently hold a credential or certification from a professional coaching organization.

One of the groups training life coaches is the International Coaching Federation (ICF), whose founder, Thomas Leonard, has as good a claim as anyone to call himself the originator of the contemporary movement. He had a front seat to Erhard Seminars Training or "est," which ran workshops in the '70s that promised attendees radical personal change.

Leonard later named and claimed the territory of life coaching and held teleclasses with hundreds of coaches around the world to define the field. His friend and fellow coach Dave Buck, with whom he founded the life coach training academy CoachVille in 2000, says their vision of coaching is as an anti-hierarchical "movement towards egalitarian co-creation."[5] In the early days of coaching development in North America, Buck and Leonard talked about creating communities and accreditation: "When you have certification, you have authority, right?" This thought seems to run counter to the egalitarian ethos of coaching that Buck 's just told me about, and his own profile lists him as the seventh most influential person in the history of professional coaching. He acknowledges, somewhat cryptically, that there is a "tension between what is and future potential."

The last ICF survey estimated that there were 71,000 coaches worldwide in 2019, a 33% increase on the 2015 estimate. It might seem like there are more life coaches than the market can hold, but economic precarity, which has worsened through the pandemic, seems to have increased supply. For those who have lost jobs, it is a field that has a low barrier to entry. In one Facebook group for new life coaches that I joined out of curiosity, more than a few people say they used to be hotel managers or bartenders. Goldman says that many life coaches work part-time in other professions.

Social media has also democratized coaching, and led to its blurring with other forms of aspirational content. Sixteen-year-olds on TikTok are "manifesting," by which they meditate, reflect, set goals, then break them down. Although they might not use the label, they are something resembling a life coach to their followers.[6]

Life coaching might not address the structural problems in our society, in which too many find it difficult to attain even the base of Maslow's hierarchy of needs. But I can see its attraction for individuals stuck in the middle who want to reach the top. Near the end of my session with Birk, the language of commitment started to seep in: We're looking to "scaffold" and take "the little steps." I pledged to do things. If I'd been a regular client, in two weeks' time, she'd check that I had. Life coaching gives you the feeling that you are able to change something, if not everything else.

(5) CoachVille's website offers a pithier philosophy: "Any endeavor in life can be designed as a winnable game worth playing and coaches alone are charged with helping everyone win the game that matters most to them right now."

(6) In North America, the majority of life coaches (53%) are from the baby-boom generation. Globally, millennials account for just under one in 10 coach practitioners.

Fatima

AL QADIRI:

It was a freezing night in February 2019, and onstage in Berlin as her alter ego, Shaneera, Fatima Al Qadiri was magnificently disdainful. Over the sound of her nimble, joyous club tracks—a mutant hybrid of UK grime music and the percussion of the Persian Gulf—she flicked her long black hair with venom. I wove through the heaving nightclub crowd to get a closer look. Her face was caked in layers of stage makeup but I could still make out a distinctly bored expression. It was an act, of course, but the audience adored the music and her haughty manner. They danced away all their tiredness and the cold. As fully as she embodied the persona of Shaneera that night, the character was just one waypoint on a restless musical journey that threads avant-garde club music with a sharp stream of critical thought. Born in Kuwait in 1981, Al Qadiri has had a career that's taken her across the globe, from club gigs at Berlin techno temple Berghain to art shows at MoMA, cementing her role as a distinctly conceptual figure in electronic music. This intellectual bent made me apprehensive that she might prove intimidating in conversation. Talking on Zoom, however, she is generous and thoughtful, chatting warmly from her newly adopted home of Los Angeles.

A deep, throaty laugh punctuates her sentences as she describes her childhood. Growing up in the aftermath of the Gulf War, she hardly ever went outside. Instead, she surrounded herself with tools for inward escape: her beloved video games; anime and manga from Japan; the lavish illustrations in the books collected by her artist mother; a deep reservoir of vivid daydreams. Such distractions would later serve as more than just entertainment: they would become talismans to be interrogated, reinterpreted and recontextualized across her career. For Al Qadiri the young girl, though, they simply helped while away the blazing afternoons in

Words
TOM FABER

Photography
JUSTIN CHUNG

Kuwait. “Our house had this empty roof at the top,” she recalls. “The buildings around were low so you had this massive horizon and I would sit there after school, listening to my CD Walkman for hours, just reading and daydreaming.”

Music-making first entered her life via a Casio keyboard she found in her house as a child. “I started writing music as a nine-year-old to express myself. I didn’t feel comfortable with words: My Arabic wasn’t good, I was more comfortable in English but it was still foreign.” Al Qadiri attended a British school because her father thought it would mean she could avoid a state-indoctrinated education, but Arabic was taught only as a second language. Her parents spoke the Kuwaiti Arabic dialect at home, but this was quite different from the classical, written Arabic used across the Arab world. While English felt simpler and more contemporary to her, it was always distinctly foreign. “I was troubled by my linguistic relationship to my identity, so I used music to express that. It became my first language, my diary.”

A few days after her ninth birthday in 1990, Saddam Hussein appeared on TV to announce that Iraq was going to invade Kuwait. His forces entered the country on August 2 and occupied it until they were pushed back by US-led coalition forces in early 1991. Al Qadiri’s diplomat father and artist mother both operated as members of the Kuwaiti resistance, printing a newsletter of dissent that put them on the invaders’ hit list. The family moved house repeatedly to avoid being tracked down by the military. Her father once arrived 30 minutes late to a Kuwaiti resistance meeting to discover that everyone who arrived on time had been murdered. He was later taken to a concentration camp in Basra for around two months. “My parents almost got executed so many times,” she says. “They really shouldn’t still be alive.”

THE SHAPESHIFTING STAR OF CONTEMPORARY ELECTRONICA.

Styling
NATASHA NEWMAN-THOMAS

Hair & Makeup: Nicole Wittman, Photo Assistant: Dylan Pearce

When her father was taken to the concentration camp, she wasn't home because she had gone to a friend's house to play a new video game. For the first months of the conflict, she didn't quite understand what was going on and was simply happy to be skipping school.

Her musical breakout 22 years later, the *Desert Strike* EP, plays on these contrasts between childhood innocence and the visceral realities of war. It is named for a video game released soon after the invasion, in which players are cast as an American pilot flying a helicopter over an unnamed country in the Persian Gulf, single-handedly repelling terrorist groups. To see her traumatic recent history turned into a game horrified the young Al Qadiri. "I hated that game. It was so sinister to release it immediately after the war. I remember there was no music, just the whirr of the helicopter and the sound effects of bombs. I felt like I was plugged into virtual reality—what am I looking at? People play this to have fun? This is deranged."

Her EP was a soundtrack imagined for this game without music, drawing from grime, a strain of UK hip-hop known for its martial rhythms, raw production style and furious energy. Al Qadiri's take was more measured—melodically lush and freighted with complex ideas of personal and cultural trauma. Its glistening synths invoke the soundtracks of early video games, referencing the horror that inspired it, yet it still serves as a superb collection of club tracks. "My first existential feelings happened when I played that game," she says. "It haunted me and that's why I made the record, to release those feelings."

By the time she released *Desert Strike*, Al Qadiri was living in the US, where she had moved at 17 to go to college. She had accessed a music production studio at 19 during a composition course at the University of Miami, and her earliest releases infused contemporary club sounds with the sonic textures of her home. There was the *Muslim Trance Mix*, released under the name Ayshay, which sampled Islamic devotional songs over austere drums and a synthesized choir, followed by another Ayshay record of vocal compositions in a similar vein, before the tropical sounds of her club-focused *Genre-Specific Xperience* EP.

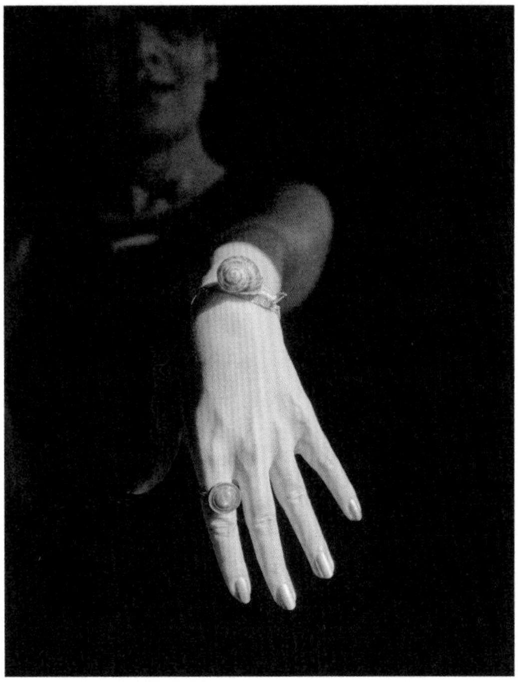

(above)
Al Qadiri wears a vintage necklace and bracelet by VIVIENNE WESTWOOD and a ring by ALICE CICOLINI at August LA.

But it was *Desert Strike* that put Al Qadiri on the musical map in 2012, attracting the interest of UK label Hyperdub, which has been at the vanguard of forward-thinking electronic music for over 15 years. This has been the home of her last four records; though she has received requests to produce for mainstream artists and "go pop," she has yet to accept. "I'm just not pop material," she says with a deep laugh. "I'll always be a cult bitch, you know, forever."

Her debut full-length album, 2014's *Asiatisch*, also carried an intellectual framework. Inspired by her love of the Chinese poetry she studied at college and the Black musicians in Europe and the States who referenced Chinese melodies and instruments in their music—from the Wu-Tang Clan's fascination with kung fu films to London's "sinogrime" producers—Al Qadiri created her own paean to an imagined China, a country she had never visited.

It was at once beautiful and strange, composed of bright melodies and hollow drums made using her music software's default "Asian" sound kit, the concept examining racist stereotypes of Chinese culture ranging from *Lady and the Tramp* to the idea of China as a home for cheap imitation goods. The opening track foregrounds a garbled Chinese cover of "Nothing Compares 2 U" backed by a choir of synthesized celestial voices. It sounds strained, thin and curiously captivating. Al Qadiri's music was becoming more concerned with its own digital nature, each release a dizzying hall of mirrors.

These same themes returned to Al Qadiri when she was bedbound nursing a knee injury in Kuwait in early 2015, watching the protests half a world away in Baltimore following the death of Freddie Gray, a 25-year-old Black man in police custody, so soon after the protests around the fatal shooting of Michael Brown by police officer Darren Wilson in Ferguson, Missouri. She was experiencing violence through the lens of the media, and it ignited the explicitly

(left) Al Qadiri wears clothes by MAISON MARGIELA throughout the shoot.

political side of her personality partly inherited from her parents. It also made her reflect on the first protest she had attended after arriving in the United States. "The minute I landed in America I saw the brutal suppression of a protest against the World Trade Organization and the World Bank in DC in September 1999." This was a deep shock, nothing like the country she had expected to find. "Here I was coming wide-eyed and naive to the US, thinking this is a progressive country. All the goddamn democracy propaganda I've been fed all my life about the States, and then I've never witnessed a larger police presence. I felt I was fed some Kool-Aid, thinking you could protest, that you had freedom of assembly in this country."

The right to protest, which Al Qadiri's parents had always taught her was as important as freedom of speech, became the subject of her next album, *Brute*, released in 2016 with a picture of a Teletubby wearing riot gear on the cover. Musically, it was perhaps familiar to listeners of her previous work, but this record was differentiated by the sounds of breaking glass, gunshots and a sample of ex-LAPD Sergeant Cheryl Dorsey speaking about the lack of accountability in the US police system.

I comment on how rare it is that artists in electronic music have such rigorous thematic frameworks for each release. Al Qadiri laughs. "Yes, my ideas are relatively elaborate," she says. "I put out a small manifesto for each record." It is impressive then, that her music rarely buckles under its conceptual weight. "I don't think it matters if people read my ideas behind the records. They're either going to like the album or they won't," she says. "Ultimately the connection is with the music."

By the time I saw Al Qadiri perform for the first time, on that winter night in 2019, she had perfected the union of music and concept. She was performing tracks from her 2017 record *Shaneera*, for which she had assumed a persona—and aesthetic—inspired by her friends in the queer scene and the Arab pop divas of the 2000s. "These were straight women with so much makeup they could give drag queens a run for their money," she says. "I wanted to play with that border between what is drag and what isn't—this extreme femininity. Shaneera is a persona that can embody any person. She's an evil queen, and she's fab."

The record was her loosest and most ebullient yet, made in collaboration with queer Kuwaiti friends and including quotes sourced from Grindr conversations. Her mother stood over her, listening to drafts of the tracks, telling her when she was going too far and might cause problems in conservative Kuwaiti society. "I had to censor the shit out of this record," she says. After the release of *Shaneera*, friends from around the Arab world sent her videos of people at queer parties dancing to her music. "That's the highest compliment I could get from this record," she says. "The girls were listening to it!"

Though she grew up in Kuwait, Al Qadiri was born in Dakar, Senegal, where her father worked as a diplomat before the family returned to Kuwait when she was two. She has never been back to the country of her birth, but it felt more than mere coincidence when French-Senegalese director Mati Diop asked Al Qadiri to write the score for her debut film, *Atlantics*, a strange and atmospheric ghost story set in Dakar that won the Grand Prix at Cannes in 2019. Al Qadiri's soundtrack showcased her music at its most tender and eerie, her rumbling bass echoing Diop's long, ambiguous shots of the sea. "The opportunity really changed my life," she says. "It's been a lifelong dream of mine to score a film."

And so she moves from project to project, each a fascinating prism of ideas and a new canvas for her singular sound. When I ask about her latest album, *Medieval Femme*, released in early 2021, I am not surprised to learn that she is once again returning to the subject of her childhood. Around the age of 11, when she was spending a lot of time inside the house, she had fallen into a serious depression, unable to go to school or even get out of bed. "This was when I started having really intense daydreams to escape reality. I was like: *Okay, I'm getting expelled, I don't know how to deal with this*, so I just daydreamed all day and ignored the pain. I started having these elaborate time-traveling historical Medieval fantasies, imagining myself as a man in a lot of them. Growing up in Kuwait as a girl in a male-dominated society... by age 11, I knew it was a disadvantage to be a woman in this culture."

Al Qadiri later read a collection of classical Arabic poetry written by women and was taken aback by the sensuality and sometimes explicit sexuality she found, which stood in sharp contrast to the taboo around female sexual desire in much of the Arab world today. "I got this sense of very extreme melancholic longing," she says. "These women *wanted* so much. Almost all their poetry was demands, requests, needs that were not being fulfilled. It got me thinking about the relationship between desire and depression, and how the two coincided in my own life. I started to view depression as a state of extreme longing and desire, where desire stops you in your tracks and you can't move or even function because you *want* so much."

Her daydreams and poetic readings coalesced into *Medieval Femme* (an album Al Qadiri refers to using the pronoun "she") which envisions a walk through a daydream of an Islamic garden. It is a sonic departure from *Shaneera*, leaning into synthesized approximations of music from the Middle Ages, both Arabic and European. "This album is a mood that possesses you and takes you somewhere where desire, depression, pain and sensual longing coincide," she explains. This is audible in both Al Qadiri's own plaintive vocals, featured more prominently than in any of her recent work, and in the lack of rhythms, replaced here by yawning, empty spaces between melodies.

The record's striking cover design is taken from an artwork by Al Qadiri's mother, Thuraya Al-Baqsami. Entitled *Message 1*, it was painted in 1990, two weeks before the invasion of Kuwait.[1] In the image, a woman is set against a deep indigo background, wearing an enigmatic expression. She is delivered a message by a bird while a dark cloud gathers overhead. "My mom had a bad feeling," Al Qadiri says. "She's a total psychic actually, she reads fortunes. Every time I go to Kuwait she reads the grounds of my coffee. In this image, I fell in love with the woman's face. There is no iris in her eye so she seems completely inaccessible—it's how a depressed person is, like a shell. You know there's a person in there, but you can't get through to them."

While making the album, Al Qadiri moved from Berlin, her home of four years, to Los Angeles. She spent her first year there in isolation due to the COVID-19 pandemic, which was okay for the most part. She describes her personality as "pretty lazy, like a house cat," so she was relatively content to sit at home playing retro-style video games. "They reconnect me with my childhood," she says. "I just want to be in my pajamas, drinking fruit juice and eating psychotic amounts of candy. I want to be transported back to this fetal position of playing a game in a more innocent time."

Her new house has a garden and a hiking trail around the corner. "It's this quiet, leafy suburb," she says, "a cute Mexican neighborhood surrounded by hills with trees and flowers I've never seen before in my life. It's very green and lush and beautiful, and somehow it's fate, you know?"

Al Qadiri talks about fate a lot. She says it's fate that her mother created her portentous work a matter of days before the invasion of Kuwait, that she ended up scoring a film made in her birth city of Dakar, and that at the time she releases an album about a walk through a garden, she has arrived in a new home surrounded by nature. She uses the Arabic expression, "Kitabak maktūb": *Your book has already been written.*

I ask what "fate" means to her. "Fate is circumstances that lead you to go down the path of your life," she says. So does that mean she doesn't have free will to make choices in her life? Al Qadiri thinks for a moment. "I think you do make choices, but those choices still take you down that same road. Free will is the day-to-day reality, fate is the long-term path."

"I believe it is my destiny to be a musician," she says firmly. Music has become a necessity in her life: it is her native language, a repository for her memories, a space to externalize and interrogate her ideas. Her life could not have gone any other way. "The day I stop composing I must have lost the will to live, or have extreme arthritis, or maybe it's reached the point that I can no longer even hum a melody," she says. "Only death will stop me from writing music."

(1) Al Qadiri recalls one particular moment which highlighted the constant danger posed to her family at that time. "My mom was stopped at a checkpoint once by a 17-year-old with a Kalashnikov," she says. "He searched her car and found a camera, which, because it contained politically sensitive photographs, was a crime punishable by death." Al Qadiri's mother was saved by her quick thinking: "She said, 'I promise, if you don't report me, I'll take you to Paris when this is all done.'"

(right) Al Qadiri wears a vintage bracelet by VIVIENNE WESTWOOD and a top and sweater by MAISON MARGIELA.

“ The day I stop composing I must have lost the will to live, or have extreme arthritis.”

LOEWE
KOMPERDELL

Pack a bag.
Pitch a tent.
Find a slice of nature
to call your own.

83

OFF GRID

Photography
MARINA DENISOVA
Styling
JUAN CAMILO
RODRÍGUEZ

(previous) Clara wears a vintage top from LA COMUNE in Barcelona, shorts by LORENZO MARTINEZ and a scarf by LE ARTELIER. Daniel wears a shirt by DRIES VAN NOTEN, shorts by MISSONI and a belt by LOEWE.
(below) Daniel wears a vintage shirt from LA COMUNE in Barcelona.

(below)　Belt by LOEWE.

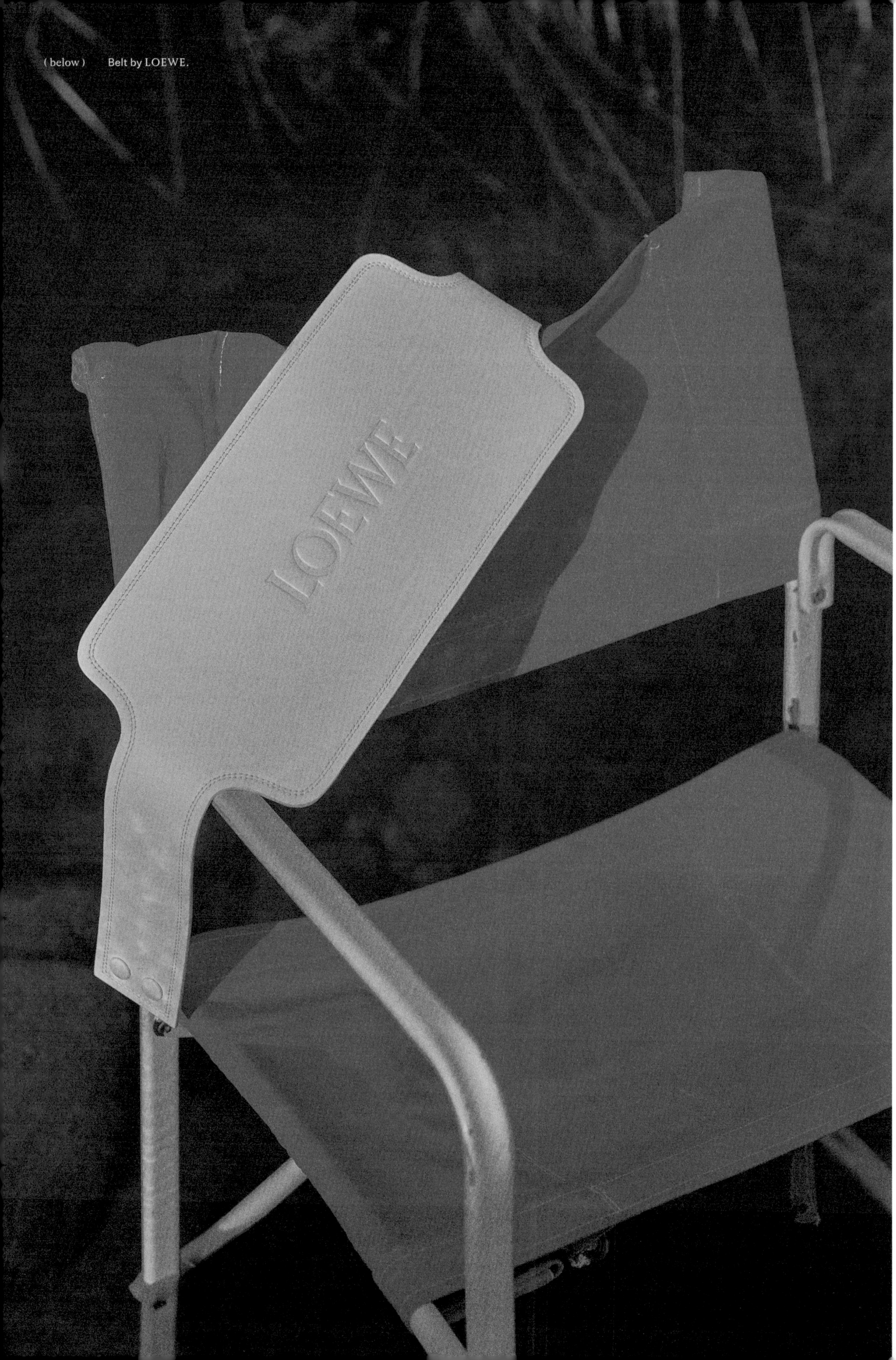

(below) Clara wears a shirt by COURRÈGES and a skirt and shoes by LOEWE.

(above) Clara and Daniel wear outfits by WEDÚ.

(above) Clara wears a cardigan by LOEWE and a vintage skirt from LA COMUNE in Barcelona.

(below) Daniel wears a top by A.P.C.

Set Design
SOMMET STUDIO
Set Design Prep
LAURA DOARDO
Hair & Makeup
NIKA AMBROŽIČ
Production
EQUIPO SEA & MOUNTAIN EXPERIENCE

Models
DANIEL CALVO &
CLARA DENISON at Elite Spain
Location
RIERA DE VILARDELL

STUDIO TOUR: Fernando Caruncho

Gardens sit between the natural and the artificial. George Upton meets the man mediating between the two.

Photography
CHRISTIAN MØLLER ANDERSEN

From his peaceful Spanish studio, FERNANDO CARUNCHO has dreamt of gardens made of pine forests, wheat fields and vineyards—then gone out and made them.

From Fernando Caruncho's desk, he looks out across dusty wheat fields to the mountains north of Madrid that were once painted by Velázquez. Framed by the double doors of the "kiosk"—a small pavilion where the landscape designer and his team meet to discuss projects from Florida to New Zealand—is a perspective typical of Caruncho's work over the past 40 years: restrained, sober gardens merging seamlessly with the landscape and the vast changing sky of the Sierra de Guadarrama.

When he came to the site 20 years ago, it was this view that informed the design of the studio and its gardens—the "point of gravity," as he describes it, around which the square, cream-colored buildings and the immaculate rows of boxwood and laurel were arranged. Now 62, Caruncho oversees a team of 12 that includes his sons, Pedro and Fernando. They work in the kiosk and an office where the firm's global operations are coordinated. Between these spaces is a contemporary evocation of the gardens of antiquity that first drew Caruncho to the profession. "The Academy of Plato was a garden; the Lyceum [where Aristotle taught] was a garden; the Stoa, where the Stoic philosophers met, was in a garden," he says. "I was inspired by how being in nature created ideas."

Caruncho was a passionate reader when he was younger and studied philosophy at university in Madrid before turning to garden design. He set out without a business plan or strategy, but over the next four decades he became a highly sought-after garden designer, collaborating with architects like Pritzker Prize–winner Renzo Piano and creating relationships with clients that have endured over the years. "People are always calling us, saying they have discovered an extra couple of hectares," he mentions in passing.

Though he has found success, Caruncho is still relatively unknown. His gardens are prized for their clarity, light and formal simplicity, but such is the careful, considered process of designing a garden that the firm can only take on four or five commissions each year. For those they do accept, the client is often the deciding factor. "We never say no because of the site," Caruncho says. "All places have their beauty, even those that have been neglected. The question is the affinity with the client. We have to find a responsible owner."

Every project begins with a visit to the site, which is recreated in miniature by the studio's model makers. Caruncho will develop his vision for the garden in sketches which are then translated to the scale model—an interactive process that allows his team to experiment with the topography and structure of the project. The design is tweaked and revisions requested by the client are incorporated before the details are finalized in a book of plans that are sent to local architects.

It's a process that can take, at a minimum, a year and a half, though typically it will be a lot longer, and the firm's relationship continues after the project has finished—often they will return to replant a garden damaged by a storm or disease.[1] "The value is in the process," says Caruncho. He explains that he prefers to be described as a gardener rather than as a designer. "The idea is already there in your surroundings, you just need to cultivate it."

In most cases Caruncho will be guided by the existing garden and climate, using plants and trees that are already present at a site rather than introducing new species. When he does create structure—such as the strict rectangularity of intersecting lawn and pond in a private garden in Madrid—it is part of a geometry that humanizes the garden, offering a way for people to place themselves in relationship with the landscape. It's an idea embodied most fully by his design for an island off the coast of Maine that had become overrun by pine trees. There, Caruncho simply removed certain trees to open up perspectives to the sea and give access to the natural gardens of moss and lichens.

(above)
Caruncho creates scale models of every garden project so that his team can visualize the topography of the space when designing.

Caruncho works instinctively, and it can often be a month after he has visited a site before he is inspired to put pen to paper. But this creative response is always articulated through a sense of order—the "grammar" that he says took the first 10 years of his career to learn. In southern Italy, for example, where Caruncho planted vines in rows that curve in graceful waves, he took inspiration from his visit to the vineyard in winter. Watching the snow fall from the *masseria*, Caruncho had the "incredible impression of music." It was an experience that he mediated through the demands of the site—the orientation of the vines in relation to the sun, the requirements of the vineyard's machinery—to create a landscape that is simple and lyrical. It took four years and saw Caruncho recognized as an honorary member of the prestigious Academy of Art and Drawing in Florence.

More than formal precision, it is an understanding of a garden as a medium between humans and nature that defines Caruncho's work. As he says, it is a broad definition that includes anything from "a balcony with two pots or a vase in a window" to an "agricultural garden" of neat, square parterres planted with wheat, as he created in Catalonia. His designs typically blur the boundary between the private space of the garden and the open expanse beyond. The dense grouping of plants and the empty lawns are all part of a composition that includes the valleys, mountains and the sky; his minimal palette harmonizes with the full spectrum of the natural world.

As a child, Caruncho would spend summers at his grandfather's house in Ronda, a town in southern Spain set vertiginously above a deep gorge. He recalls looking out through the railings where the ground suddenly drops away, his eyes wide as he took in the dry Andalusian landscape. "My passion for a lot of things in my life began in that view from the cliff," he says, "in trying to understand that incredible place." For the philosopher-gardener, this is at the heart of the question that runs through all his work: What is humanity's place within the natural world? After 40 years, hundreds of projects around the globe and numerous awards, has he found the answer?

"It is a universal question," he says, "but one that has never been more important to ask than now. The garden has always been a place beyond the political, beyond religion, beyond the difference between people. I worry that the relationship between humanity and the natural world has changed, that we are only relating to it in a scientific way. The only way we can continue is to return to the garden."

(1) In the early 2010s, Caruncho's own home garden was decimated by a fungal disease that he unwittingly introduced via a specimen of the South American shrub *Escallonia macrantha*. "It is a fabulous plant," he told *Architectural Digest* in 2016, "but the ones I bought came with infections that destroyed the garden's immune system."

(opposite) This building, known as the "kiosk," is where Caruncho does much of his solo work.

(above) Caruncho's study contains books on both nature and philosophy—which he studied at university in Madrid.
(opposite) The high-ceilinged reception room is used for meetings with clients.

(left)
The architecture was designed principally to work with the garden and to frame the perspective of the mountains, with the purpose of each space decided on only later. The model room, for example, originally housed a collection of orange trees.

(below) Geometry and water are both critical to Caruncho's work.
(opposite) Caruncho's interiors are a minimalist match for his gardens. He says this is a consequence of most of his work being in the Mediterranean, where the climate and light work better with bold, simple colors.

Erchen CHANG: BIGGER, BETTER, BAO-IER.

Words
APOORVA SRIPATHI

The uses Erchen Chang has found for bao might surprise you. For a Simone Rocha Christmas dinner in 2019, she created a bronzed turkey, sculpted entirely out of bao and filled with deep-fried mince pies. For a horror film–themed dinner for Hato Press in the same year, she fashioned a halibut from bao and made a performance out of "filleting" it. "All the guests took a piece home to have the next day," recalls Chang, creative director of Bao London, speaking from her home in the British capital. "That's kind of twisting people's minds a little bit, but not too much—there's warmth. There's a feeling of entering someone else's world, and that excites me."

Few people—chefs or artists—could achieve the same level of creativity through dough. Bao is, after all, not known for being a precise medium. Like other bread doughs, it requires careful kneading, proofing and shaping, not to mention steaming, which is how bao is cooked. "Bao is one of the hardest mediums to work with," says Chang. "When it's steamed the form changes, so you need to predict where it's going to go." As much as skill and technique are required, so too is patience. As Chang puts it, you need the "experience of understanding the dough."

Photography
PELLE CRÉPIN

Chang's talent is the result of an unusual path into the restaurant industry. Before her current role as the creative director of Bao, a wildly successful group of restaurants in London that she started along with her husband, Shing Tat Chung, and his sister, Wai Ting Chung, in 2013, she had already experimented with wood, clay, bronze, cloth and ceramics as an artist. Chang and Chung met, in fact, at London's Slade School of Fine Art where Chang was studying sculpture and media, focusing on performance and installation art.[1] Her final installation, "Rules to be a Lonely Man," would later become Bao's conceptual core. The piece was inspired by the classic image of the salaryman in Japanese popular culture—an overworked city dweller in an ill-fitting suit—and evolved into the restaurant's logo of a lonely man with hunched shoulders wolfing down a bao.

"The lonely man transformed into someone fatter, and slowly he had a bao in his hand, which then informed the beginning of the world building of Bao," says Chang, whose creative background—she isn't a trained chef—and Taiwanese heritage inform her perspective on both the food and restaurant aesthetics.

Picturing all the restaurants in which the lonely man might eat became key to how Chang envisioned new ventures around London: Bao Soho opened in 2015; Bao Fitzrovia in 2016; the teahouse Xu in 2017; Bao Borough, housing the group's first karaoke room, in 2019; Cafe Bao in the midst of the pandemic in 2020; and Bao Noodle Shop in Shoreditch earlier this year. All this is a long way from where the trio began eight years ago, at a stall in a parking lot in East London, selling their signature steamed milk buns with braised pork.

Today, Bao is an entire universe—or, as Chang prefers, "Baoverse." The lonely man still informs the dining experiences and the restaurants' "spaces and small details—from single diner seats to the whiskey shelf." Chang counts movies and TV among her creative inspirations, including the Japanese cartoon *Chibi Maruko Chan* and the work of directors Seijun Suzuki and Aki Kaurismäki. "They have an attention to detail and an eye for aesthetics, and their world building is amazing," she says.

At Bao, Chang's world is an homage to Taiwanese culture. "The Noodle Shop is white tiles, metal kitchens, and every surface is wipeable," says Chang. "In Soho, it's all wooden with a terrazzo floor. You may not have been to Taiwan, but when you go, you can pick out these elements," she says. "You might also think, *What Bao does is nothing like Taiwan*."

The nuances of this sort of cultural transfer have always interested Chang. "In Taiwan, you can get a cheese and ham sandwich, but there might be sweet mayo, and sweet whipped butter. In Taiwan, that's 'Western style' food, but someone from the West won't recognize it," she explains. "What is my take? We're interested in bringing a slice of Taiwanese culture to London... but at the same time, we've lived in London for a long time. We're not just recreating Taiwanese food; we are creating Bao the world."

When Chang talks about bao, the joy in her eyes is unmistakable. "It's such a big thing in my life right now; a way of expressing

(1) Shing Tat Chung, Chang's husband, is also a trained artist whose works feature in the Bao universe and the couple's home. An oil painting by Chung of three round bellies hangs above the dining table. His previous projects include creating a robot that follows the whims of lucky numbers to trade real money on the stock market.

(left)
Chang occasionally sculpts in more durable material. For Bao's merchandise, she has designed a limited edition teardrop-shaped teapot and bao-shaped candles.

"Bao is one of the hardest mediums. When it's steamed the form changes, so you need to predict where it's going to go."

myself," she says. "Bao is such an interesting form—there is so much potential to it. It has a very short life. What can I do to explore that more?"

The sculptures that she has made for *Kinfolk* spring from the same "imagination hub" as her businesses. "There's things we do for fun, to explore the form, boundaries and the limitations of bao as a medium," says Chang. Artists such as Max Ernst and Barbara Hepworth are among Chang's inspirations for the pieces pictured: "Modernists and surrealists who take pictures with their sculptures like I did. It's such an interesting relationship between the sculpture and [the artist], where the sculpture is very much reflective of their lives," she says. "This series is also reflective of my life."

The sculptural bao series is reflective of the world that Chang has built—the one that she is so passionate about, and which unites her own output with that of her icons. When she started Bao along with Shing and Wai Ting, no one in London really knew what a gua bao [pork belly bun] was, says Chang. "No one talked about it or used it." Today, bao can be found across British supermarkets in various iterations, and even in restaurants that don't serve Taiwanese food.

Does she ever consider moving on to something entirely new? Chang says she would consider it, but for now she is happy with her medium and with lovingly crafting a world around it. "There needs to be some sort of love for it in the first place."

(left) The bao teacup is reminiscent of another impractical sculpture: Méret Oppenheim's 1936 fur-covered tea set, *Le Déjeuner en fourrure*.

114 — 176

PT. 1 SILICON VALLEY.

1.0

Anna Wiener

(PROFILE)

Anna Wiener was on the path to Silicon Valley success. Then she pivoted. *Allyssia Alleyne* charts the making of a tech-skeptic.

Words
ALLYSSIA ALLEYNE
Photos
KOURTNEY
KYUNG SMITH

The Anna Wiener story, Anna Wiener warns, is not a hero's journey. "In a book, you really want your protagonist to have a specific goal: You want to see them try and fail to reach it, and then eventually either triumph or walk away, right?" she says. "But I've always just sort of followed what has looked interesting to me."

And yet in *Uncanny Valley*, Wiener's 2020 memoir about her experience working customer support roles at Silicon Valley start-ups in her 20s, she makes for a compelling protagonist. Not a hero exactly, but an astute stand-in for the consumer for whom the tech ecosystem is merely, as she writes, "the scaffolding of everyday life"—ubiquitous and useful, if not particularly well understood.

Over the course of the book, Wiener recounts swapping the New York publishing industry for venture capital–funded companies obsessed with growth metrics and fueled by a cocktail of idealism, EDM and biohacking nootropics. Accustomed to the indignities of low-paid cultural work, she's seduced by the perks of the tech sector—the comped nights out and trips to Tahoe, the full-coverage insurance and six-figure salaries. Despite herself, Wiener enjoys a type of corny corporate pride that her former self would have balked at, wearing branded swag as she and her cohorts terrorize San Francisco on bar crawls and team-building scavenger hunts.

But with time, her idealism fades into disillusionment and alarm. As a woman and non-technical worker, her soft skills are both maligned and exploited—first at "the analytics startup" and later at "the open-source startup," GitHub. (In the book, companies are routinely referred to with oblique descriptions—Amazon is "the online superstore"; Facebook is "the social network everyone hated.")

She finds it increasingly difficult to ignore the proliferation of hate speech, propaganda and misinformation on the platform (particularly during the rise of Donald Trump in 2016), and the toxic, bullying culture that festers in the workplace. Having learned firsthand how easily companies could track and access private user data, Wiener becomes paranoid about digital surveillance—not about the act of data collection itself, she writes, "but the people who might see it on the other end—people like me. I never knew with whom I was sharing my information." The book is insidery without being dishy, and eye-opening without scaremongering, pulling back the curtain on an industry many of us support but know little about.

When we speak in late August, Wiener, now 34, is sitting in her dad's office at her childhood home in Brooklyn, visiting family for the first time since the pandemic broke in 2020. I'd suggested a variety of apps for our interview, vetting each for security and encryption bona fides, but it turns out there was no need to overthink it. "I'm on all the chat/voice apps," she reassured me via email. Wiener's laptop is broken, so we speak over WhatsApp. She texts photos of her dad's "museum of obsolete technology" stacked on the desk in front of her to set the scene—a RadioShack TRS-80 microcomputer from the late 1970s, an Apple QuickTake digital camera from the mid-'90s, a Sharp minidisc recorder. A business journalist turned financial advisor, he reported on the tech industry in the 1980s and early '90s for *Fortune* and *U.S. News*. ("In the early '90s, he got particularly excited about desktop publishing, and began writing a monthly newsletter about mutual funds," she says. "My brother and I used to sit at the dining table and stuff and stamp the envelopes.")

Wiener grew up upper-middle class in Brooklyn before it was cool and stuck around for a while after college when it suddenly was, rolling her eyes at the hipsters who played arcade games in buzzy, overpriced bars. A graduate of a math-and-science magnet school in Manhattan that boasts four Nobel laureates as alumni, she studied sociology at Wesleyan University and considered a career in academia before settling into an assistant job at a literary agency in the city.

"I think it's a fascinating industry. You have all of the stuff of good literature."

At 25, demoralized by the low pay and professional precarity, she traded publishing for the promise of the tech industry, landing an unsuccessful three-month trial run at a now-defunct e-books start-up in New York before heading west. She arrived in San Francisco in 2013 without a plan, technical skills or apps on her phone; she left the industry five years later with a book deal and equity that would lead to a $200,000 stock payout when Microsoft acquired GitHub for $7.5 billion in 2018.

Ambition had little to do with any of it. "There's no brass ring that I'm charging for. [The question is] just, 'How can I do the most interesting work with the people who are most exciting to work with?' And for a while, that's why I stayed in tech," she explains. "I was just really happy to be there... and then when it came time for me to think strategically about making a plan [for my career], I realized I didn't want one."

Wiener first put her ambivalence about start-up culture into words in a fictionalized essay published by the literary magazine *n+1* in spring 2016, at the urging of an editor on staff. In pithy vignettes, she describes the slumping morale, casual sexism and office hierarchies; the bewildering interview processes and grandiose perks; the hubris, ambition and inexplicable optimism that keep the whole system churning.[1]

"I didn't consider work to be interesting for a very long time. Work was like the place that I sort of went to just get on the conveyor belt," she says. "[When I wrote the piece] I still had the sense that I was an outlier for feeling uncomfortable or alienated by tech culture, or start-up culture. There was nothing wrong with tech, but there was everything wrong with me." But quickly, Wiener discovered she wasn't alone. "When people read the piece and really identified with it, including people I had worked with, that was hugely gratifying. If I hadn't received that sort of encouragement from both friends and strangers who'd read it, I probably wouldn't have written the book," she says.

At the time, Wiener was still working at GitHub, and believed that "I had a long, rich career ahead of me in the tech industry." She tucked the book idea away as something for later, when she was ready to leave the industry, but the election that year pushed her to bring her timeline forward. She looked on with dread as the conspiracy theories and fascist ideology that had bubbled in GitHub repositories exploded into the mainstream. "Hoaxing and misinformation and memes, long the trappings of message-board culture, moved into the civic sphere. Trolling was a new political currency," she writes in the book's epilogue. "There was Nazi iconography in the news, and Nazi rhetoric in the Terms of Service team inbox...

(above) Wiener was photographed at the Children's Discovery Museum in San Jose, designed by Mexican architect Ricardo Legorreta.

No one was equipped to adjudicate speech for the millions of people spending their lives online."

"The project just felt a little more urgent to me," she explains when we speak. In December 2016, she started writing.

Her life in San Francisco, Wiener tells me, has changed significantly since the book was published. The 275-square-foot studio with bars on the windows that she first rented while working at the data analytics company has been swapped for a tasteful, spacious flat with built-in bookshelves, art and a standing piano, nestled at the foot of a hill with "a classic San Francisco view of the whole city." The roboticist boyfriend she introduces in the book is now her roboticist fiancé, and a wedding is imminent. She's still friends with a number of her former co-workers. While she will sometimes get nostalgic for the feeling of camaraderie and shared commitment to a goal (she only left GitHub in 2018, after selling *Uncanny Valley*, because she was uneasy writing at length about a current workplace), she has no regrets about leaving the start-ups behind.

With a former insider's knowledge and an outsider's objectivity, she now reports on Silicon Valley as a contributing writer at *The New Yorker*, writing about the trouble with Substack, the deplatforming of Donald Trump, and the politics of the gig economy; about whether tech entrepreneurs could actually usher in "a new era of transparent, trustworthy institutions and gleaming, functional infrastructure."

"I think it's a fascinating industry both on a sort of structural level and on a personal level," Wiener says. "You have all of the stuff of good literature, right? You have all these young people who are ambitious and competitive. You have a lot of disappointment, failure and passion, and sometimes things that actually do rearrange how people interact and lead their daily lives. And then on the sort of structural level, I think it's important to pay attention to tech and Silicon Valley to understand shifts in finance, in politics and in labor. There's so much material that it feels really generative, and just very exciting to me—still—as a subject of inquiry."

After all these years, she's still indifferent to apps beyond the usual communication tools, Spotify, a couple of New York–based publications, and a digital platform she uses to find hiking trails. Her Twitter profile sits dormant; her private Instagram account is mostly a depository for hyperreal food photos snapped at bodegas and restaurants. ("That's not really out of privacy concerns; I just stopped having things to say on those platforms.") She covers up her laptop camera as "baseline security hygiene," and denies apps access to her iPhone camera or microphone unless necessary. Location tracking is always switched off. "This is just really basic stuff—no one would look at my security preferences and be like, 'Wow, new ideas in play.'"

But Wiener's personal relationship with tech has shifted in other ways. Having seen the risks and rot from the inside, she's more critical in her approach to new products and the companies that fund them. "There's a certain amount of business intelligence that I just didn't have before I worked in tech, because I was sort of naive and coming from a very different industry," she explains. "It's made me think differently about the business model of certain companies, how they make their money and what behavior that might incentivize—or, if it's not behavioral, then what data they might be collecting."

From a surveillance perspective, she encourages people to do what they can to shore up their personal privacy but warns that individual action does little in the fight against companies whose business models rely on the collection and monetization of user data. "More than anything, this strikes me as an antitrust issue"—an issue of government regulation and legislation—"rather than a matter of individual responsibility, which ultimately serves the interests of said companies."

She advises a greater degree of skepticism toward new venture-backed companies that claim to be disrupting existing industries or services. "Generally speaking, tech companies are incredibly skilled at marketing," Wiener says. "What might be sold as an innovation is more often a form of regulatory arbitrage"—the circumvention of existing industry regulations.

"Many of the past decade's most successful—or, I should say, highly valued—tech companies have sought to create private infrastructure around existing social and economic processes, all while externalizing the risks. For consumers who hope to better understand the world tech companies want to build, it might help to think about what is actually being sold—and to whose benefit, and at what greater cost?"

For now, Wiener is content to be of that world rather than in it. Her work at *The New Yorker* is keeping her tapped in and fulfilled; and a film adaptation of *Uncanny Valley*, optioned by Universal Pictures in 2018, before the book was even published, is in the early stages of development. Wiener is on board as an executive producer. When we speak, she's working on an experimental narrative essay about venture capital for *n+1* and is feeling out plans for her next book—a novel.

"I'm just excited to keep covering this world. I feel very lucky to have fallen into it and discovered that it's interesting to me; it's so improbable," she says. "In some ways, it's even more interesting to be on the outside of it than it was to be in it because there is a sort of clarity, and detachment. There are so many stories to tell."

(1) The *n+1* essay that launched Wiener's writing career is a lightly fictionalized—and very funny—account of Silicon Valley disillusionment. Wiener later told *The Guardian* she was surprised by its success: "I thought that no one in literary *n+1* world would care about Silicon Valley start-ups, and that no one in Silicon Valley reads *n+1*."

PT. 2 THE SINGULARITY.

2.0

Metamorphosis

(FASHION)

Photography
MICHAEL OLIVER LOVE
Styling
LOUW KOTZE

(below) Pivot wears a balaclava, top, trousers and gloves by MERWE MODE, eyewear by OAKLEY and shoes by EUROPA ART & CO.
(previous) Bethany wears a balaclava, top and gloves by MERWE MODE.

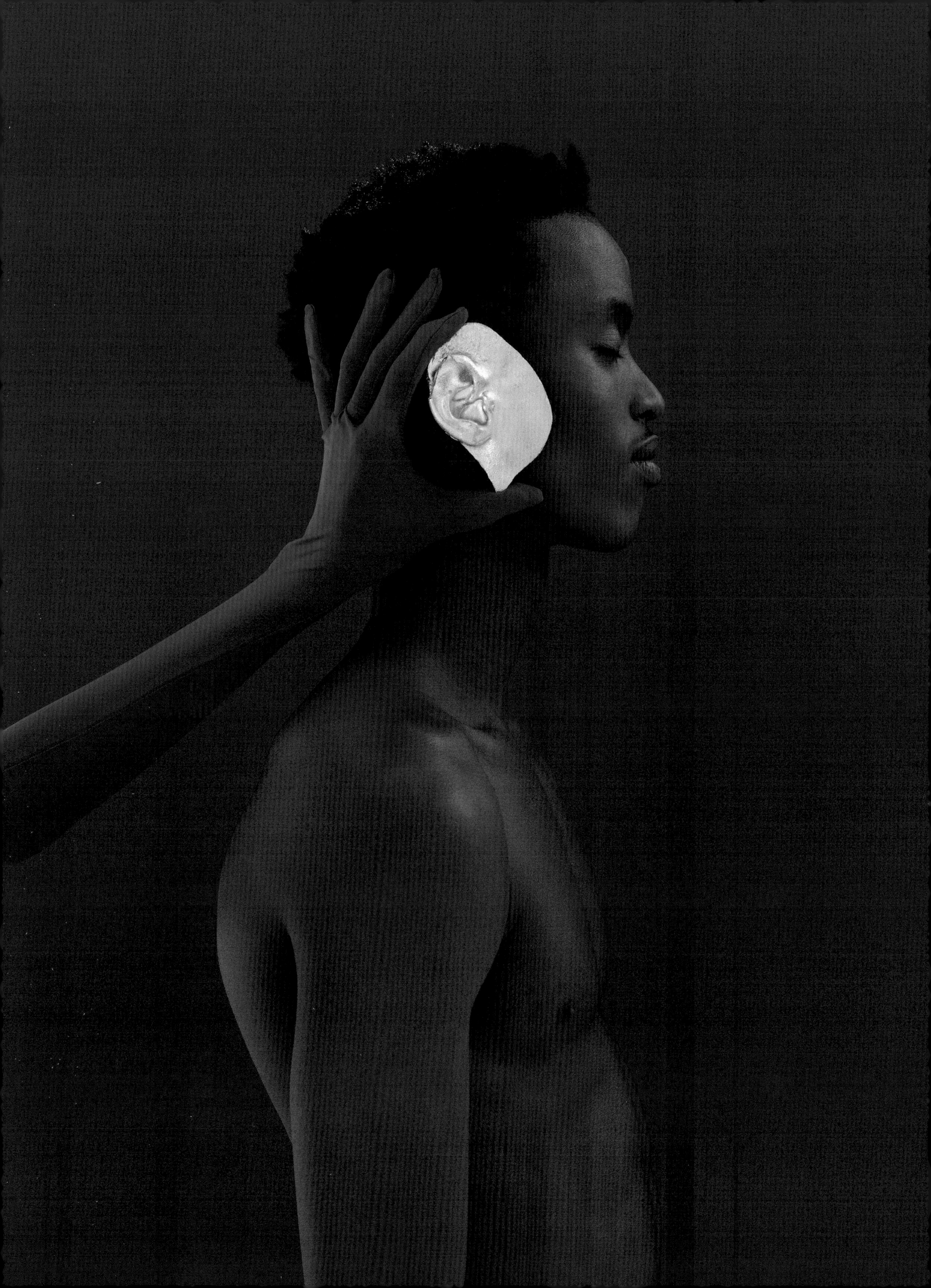

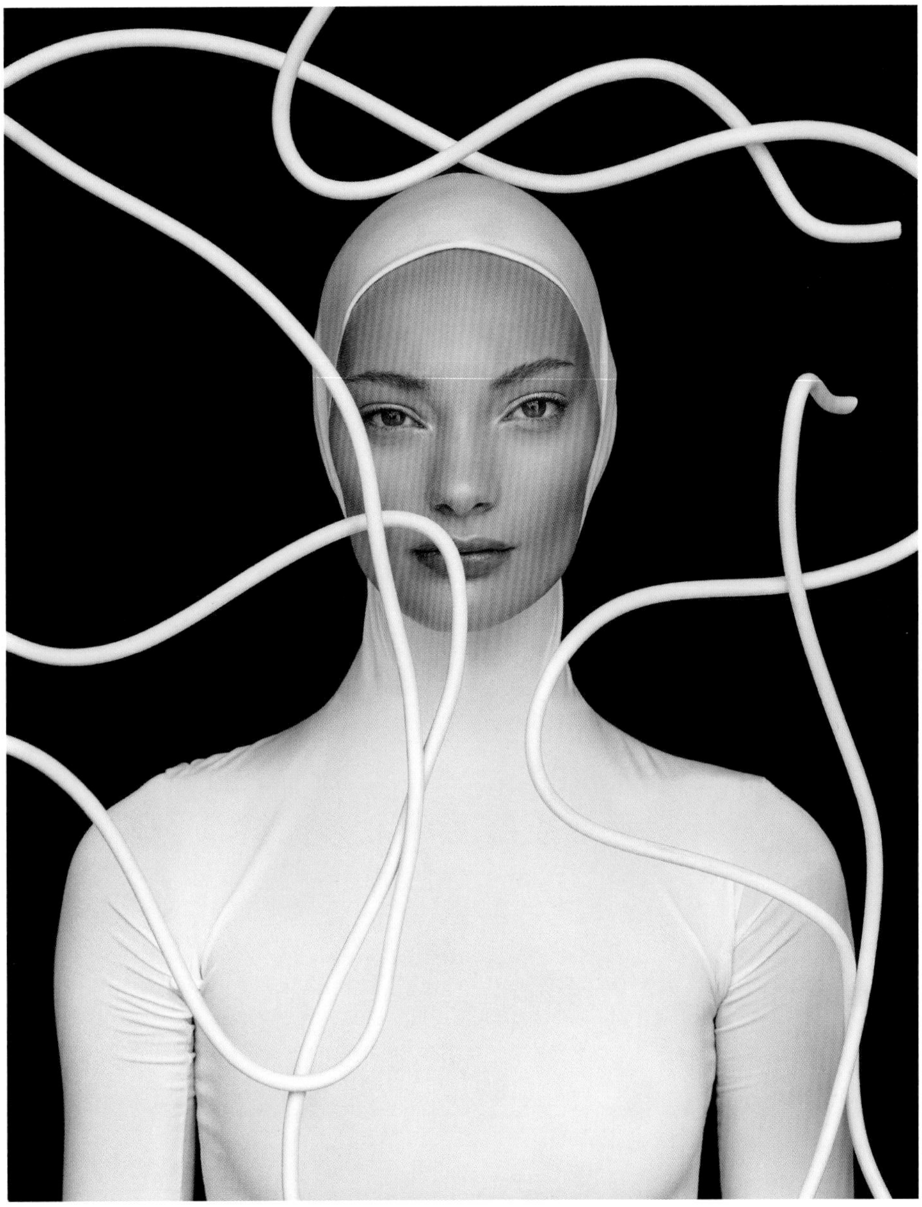

(above) Bethany wears a balaclava and top by MERWE MODE.

(below) Pivot wears a jacket and shorts by KLÛK/CGDT and shoes by EUROPA ART & CO.

(below) Pivot wears a balaclava and gloves from MERWE MODE, a jacket and trousers from VIVIERS and shoes by EUROPA ART & CO.

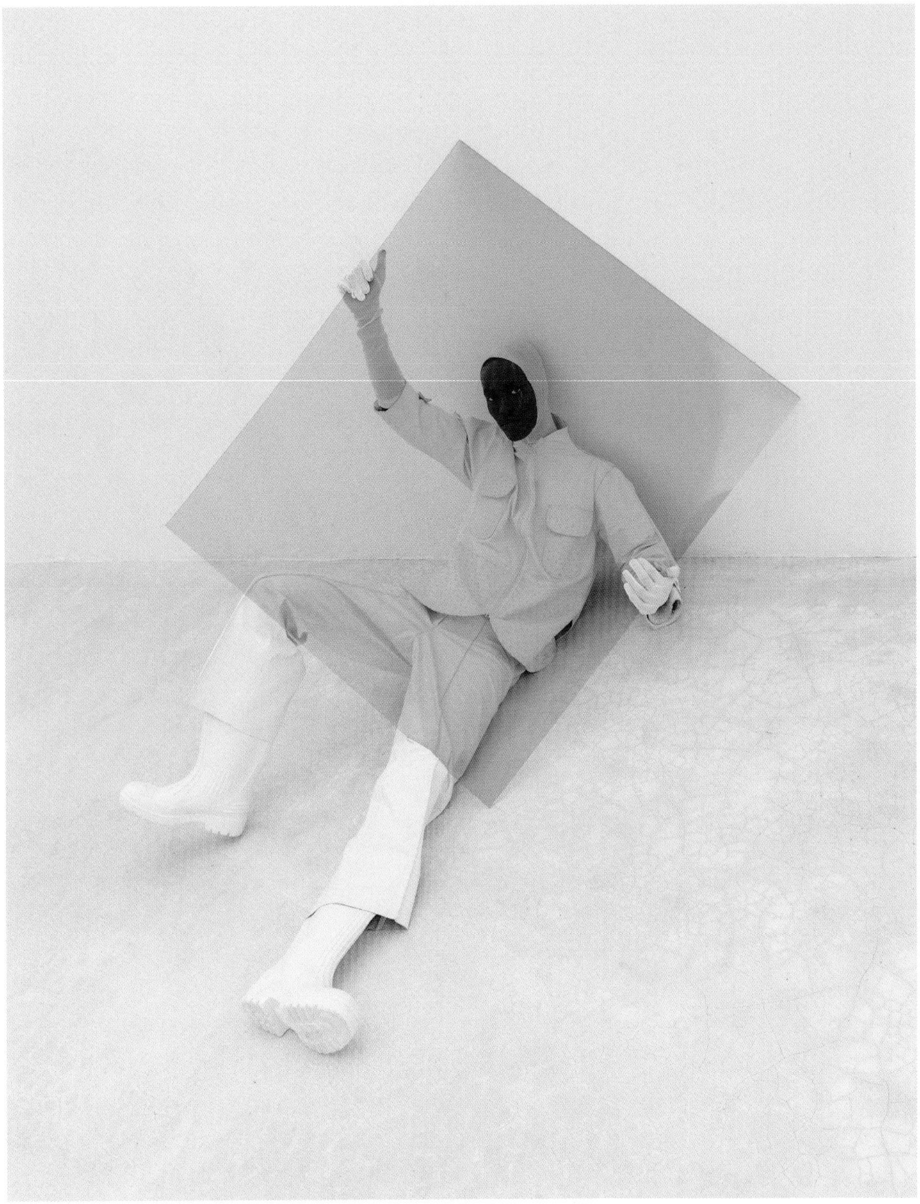

(right) Pivot wears a top, trousers, balaclava and gloves from MERWE MODE and sunglasses by OAKLEY.

(below) Bag by URBAN OUTFITTERS. Gloves by DROMEX.
(left) Pivot wears a balaclava and top from MERWE MODE and eyewear by OAKLEY.

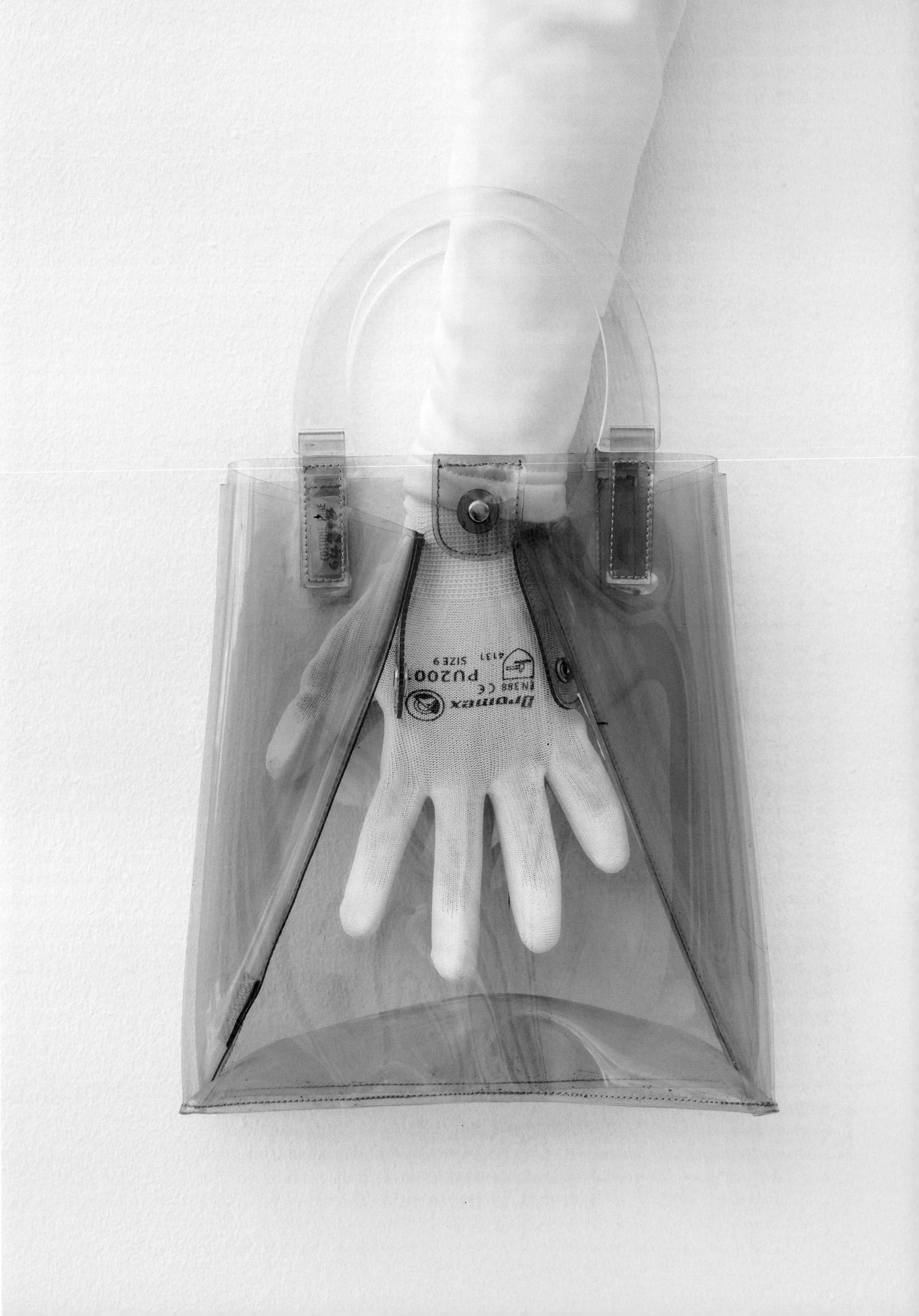

(above) Pivot wears a balaclava, gloves and top from MERWE MODE, trousers by VIVIERS and shoes from EUROPA ART & CO.
(right) Pivot wears a balaclava, trousers and gloves by MERWE MODE and a cape by GAVIN RAJAH. Bethany wears a cape and dress from GAVIN RAJAH and a balaclava and gloves by MERWE MODE.

(below) Bethany wears a balaclava and gloves from MERWE MODE, a cape and skirt from VIVIERS and shoes by EUROPA ART & CO.
(right) Pivot wears a balaclava from MERWE MODE and a jacket by VIVIERS.

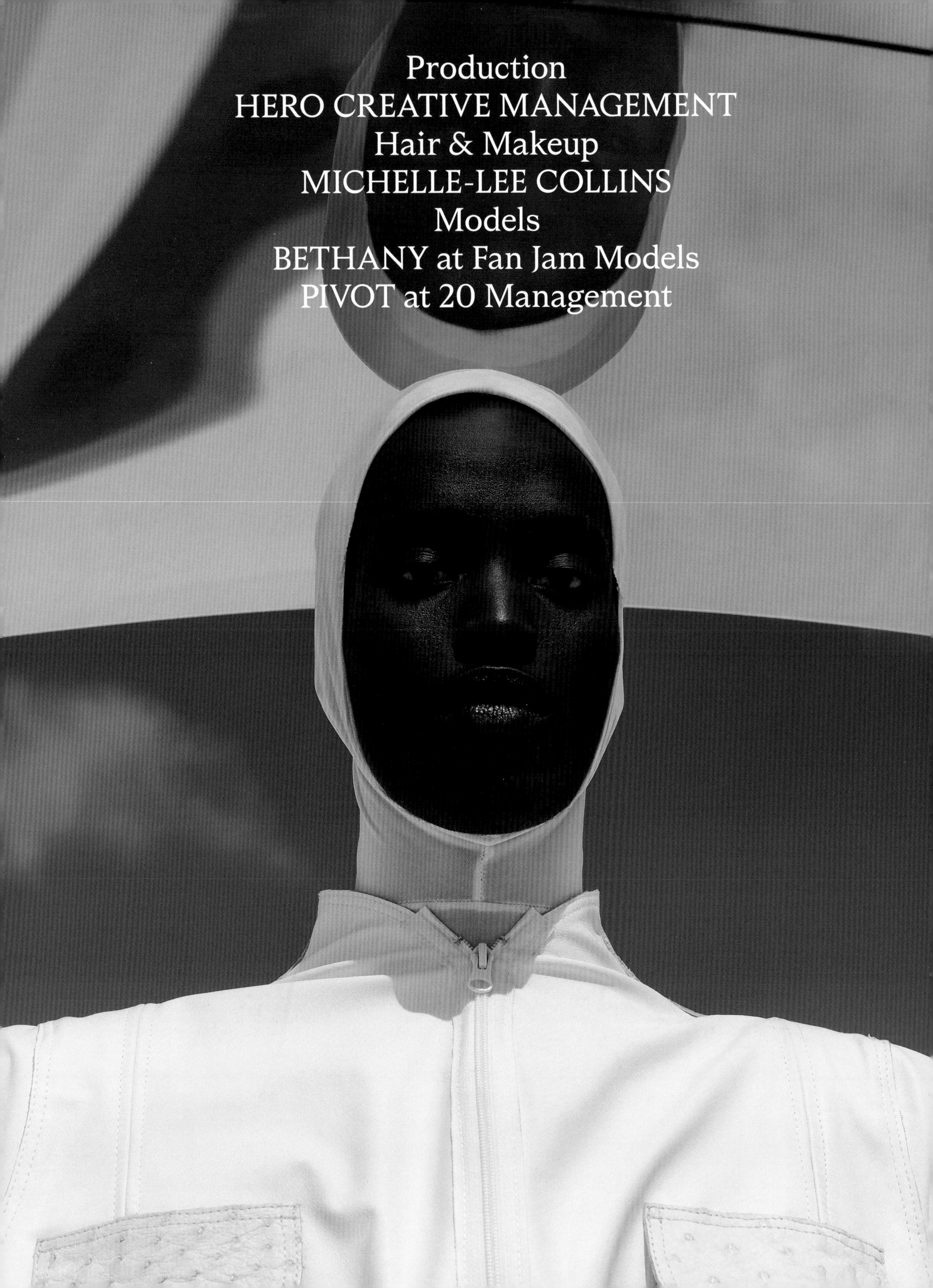

Production
HERO CREATIVE MANAGEMENT
Hair & Makeup
MICHELLE-LEE COLLINS
Models
BETHANY at Fan Jam Models
PIVOT at 20 Management

(above) Bethany wears a balaclava and gloves by MERWE MODE and eyewear by PRADA.

PT. 3
DEVICES.

Photography
GUSTAV ALMESTÅL
Set Design
ANDREAS FRIENHOLT

3.1

Custom Ringtones

(ESSAY)

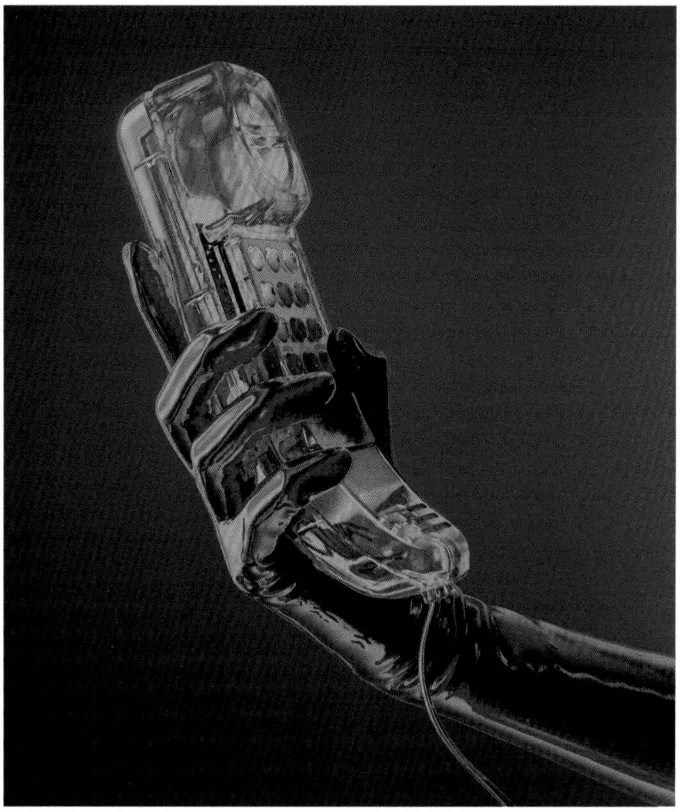

A relic forever silenced.

Every few years, reflections begin on a new batch of trends that have made the revolution from cool to uncool to historical—and then, maybe, back to cool again. Why are those kids on Instagram embracing the Juicy tracksuits that were so gauche in 2002? What about *pedal pushers*? But some trends don't get a second chance: Why, pray, did we ever spend our hard-earned money (or more likely, our parents') on ringtones for our cell phones?

When cell phones first came out, and you finally got one, you wanted to do everything you could to draw attention to it. Custom ringtones were first popularized by a nation of early tech adopters: Japan. The Digital Minimo D319, released in 1996, allowed owners to write their own custom ringtone ditties using the keypad. It was an instant smash: A book explaining how to mimic popular songs on a keypad sold over 3.5 million copies.

The first polyphonic ringtone—meaning it could play more than one note at a time—was featured on the Nokia 3510 in 2002. The advent of Truetones a few years later, actual snippets of songs rather than re-recorded versions of them, helped buoy the record industry through the Napster years. An MP3 file of a song cost 99 cents. But a fraction of the same song packaged as a ringtone could be sold for $2.99, three times as much.

In 2004, *Billboard* launched a ringtone chart, and the Recording Institute Association of America distributed Gold and Platinum records for ringtone sales for the first time in 2006. Five years later, in her "Video Phone" single, Beyoncé was offering a handsome stranger the opportunity to pick his own ringtone when she saved his number on her phone. By the end of the decade, they were a multibillion-dollar business.

With the smartphones of today, it's possible to make any song into a ringtone via Apple Music or other apps. So why is it such an eye-rolling rarity to hear a custom ringtone?

Perhaps they became cringe around the time cell phones stopped being fun and started being annoying. These days, a phone call most often means either bad news or that a robot wants to talk to you. Also, in the words of one Reddit user, a custom ringtone is a great way to start "hating your favorite song."

It seems unlikely that phones will never not be addictive, spying black holes. So maybe, unlike Juicy tracksuits, custom ringtones will stay crumpled in the dustbin of trend history.

Words
STEPHANIE D'ARC TAYLOR

3.2 Digital Hoarding

(ESSAY)

The ascendancy of virtual memory.

If a picture is worth a thousand words, then our smartphones are equipped to turn us into novelists within minutes. The average American currently has 582 photos saved on their cell phone, plus 13 unused phone apps, 83 bookmarked websites, 21 desktop icons and 210 gigabytes of cloud storage.

Digital hoarding is a sneaky problem—it's like physical hoarding, but because most of it takes place in the virtual ether, it's difficult to quantify until we start receiving cloud storage upgrade alerts or we're told we're running out of space on our phones while we're trying to take a photograph.

Amassing emails, bookmarking webpages, keeping duplicate files, maintaining text messages that date back years and taking an exorbitant number of photographs are all signs of digital hoarding.

Sound like you? It's most of us. Our cloud systems have essentially become cyber junk drawers. When a new photo is just the press of a thumb away, an email can be used as a receipt and most of our communication takes place via text, it's difficult to choose a detailed digital culling over the siren song of a simple storage upgrade. But how do we navigate all this stuff—and what does the device clutter do to our stress levels, not to mention our memories?

Technology has adapted to mitigate our data deluge. Phone and computer operating systems have installed keyword search functions for emails and text messages, and intelligent curation on smartphones arranges our best shots and alerts us to notable memories from our photo library. The demand for personal photo organizers is booming, and the work can also be offloaded onto any number of specialized apps.

Even if we're comfortable with technology or with strangers cherry-picking our most cherished digital souvenirs, the very act of taking too many pictures in order to remember a moment could be altering our ability to be in or to even recall the moment. Reliance on technology to document our lives—known as cognitive offloading—has been shown to distract us and change the way we remember experiences, because we're not truly paying attention. What we're left with are beautiful but hollow images lacking in emotional connection.

The pendulum swings both ways, though—when was the last time you memorized a phone number, wrote on a paper calendar or read a physical map? Smartphones can provide helpful cognitive shortcuts. Intentional photo taking can enhance enjoyment and leave behind cherished keepsakes for later generations. It's now up to us to draw the line at what in our lives is remembered by our physical versus virtual brains. Perhaps the phrase should be altered, for future reference: A thousand pictures are worth a digital legacy.

Words
KATIE CALAUTTI

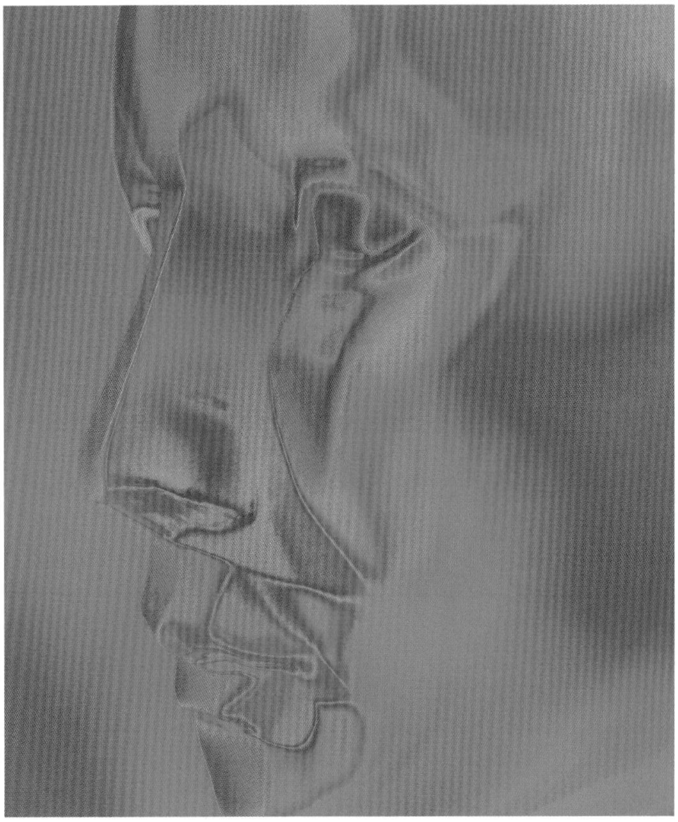

It's hard to imagine now, but the internet was once envisioned as a democratic feminist utopia—a place to escape the restrictions of a physical body. In 1991, a collective of radical feminist academics published the influential Cyberfeminist Manifesto. "The future is unmanned," they wrote, declaring themselves "saboteurs of big daddy mainframe."

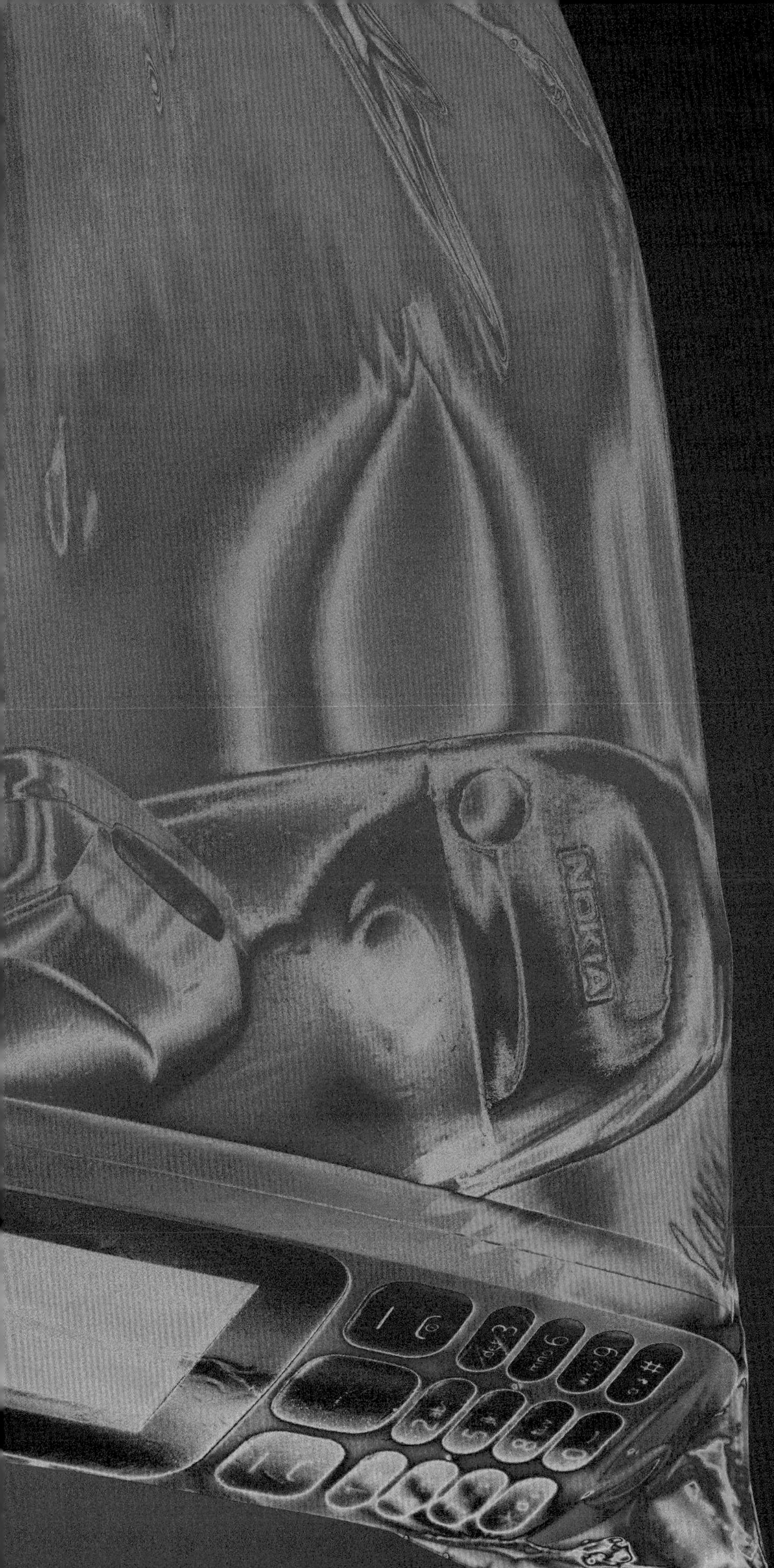
NOKIA

3.3

Dumb Phones

(ESSAY)

Words
BAYA SIMONS

An intentionally archaic device.

In 2014, back when the iPhone 5 was the hot tech of the moment, an image of Rihanna began circulating online. The singer had been photographed walking out of a bar in New York talking on a basic flip phone. It struck a chord: To see one of the most famous—and arguably coolest—women in the world rejecting constant internet connection gave the dumb phone, as they've become known, cachet.

The internet-less phone never went out of production, and in recent years, as smartphones have encroached ever more on our time, sales of old-school phones have risen in tandem, driven by a consumer desire to be less dependent on apps, 4G and Wi-Fi. The prospect might initially elicit alarm (being off-line while out of the house is becoming less and less feasible), but the rewards are unarguably appealing: The gift of extra time usually given over to scrolling through Instagram, Twitter or the news cycle; greater attention to the moment and the people around you. There's also the allure of withdrawing your data from the world, of making yourself untraceable, less constantly come-at-able for advertisers. One start-up has taken the idea of the dumb phone to the extreme. For just $12, the NoPhone—a solid plastic block—offers a handheld "surrogate" fake phone for people with screen addictions. Will our desire for connection be assuaged by a stress ball shaped like a phone? It seems unlikely.

Other companies are coming up with a middle ground. The Light Phone is a "minimal" smartphone "designed to be used as little as possible." It has no social media, news, email or internet functions, just call, SMS, a music player and an alarm. But at $299 (or $30 a month), you're essentially paying for the appearance of a smartphone with the capabilities of a Nokia 3210 (the original dumb phone) at 10 times the cost. Buying a product to solve an addiction to another product is a capitalist solution to a capitalist problem—one purposefully created by power-hungry tech companies.

Perhaps even the dumb phone is a Band-Aid over a bullet hole. After all, the world is now designed around smartphones, and unless you are Rihanna, to opt out of that system is socially and logistically self-obstructive. Until big tech is properly regulated, it's up to us to adjust our relationship to smartphones and to regain control over our own time: Delete your apps, take up a new hobby, practice not checking emails outside of working hours. You can use the smartphone—it doesn't have to use you.

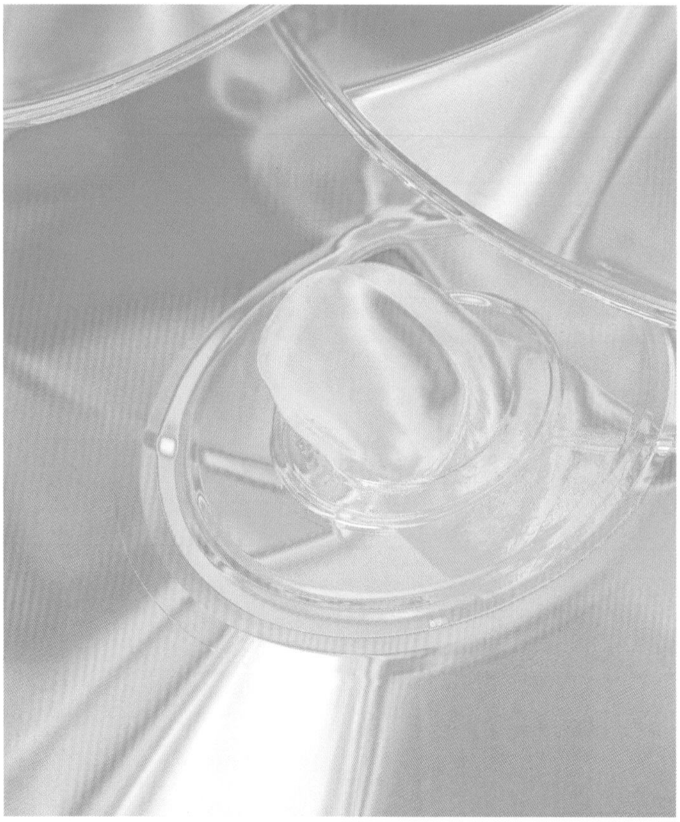

3.4
Family Chats

(ESSAY)

An all-new family institution.

Words
JOHN OVANS

Lately, visiting my parents sets my teeth on edge. Both are 70, progressively harder of hearing and prolific WhatsApp users. These elements combined mean that they have their phone notifications turned to extra loud, the noise clanging throughout the house and aggressively cutting through moments of peace. Mom marauds about with her iPhone dangling from her neck on a lanyard, shout-dictating into it as if she were sending a telegram in the 1920s: "LOVELY TO SEE YOU. PERIOD. ALL WELL HERE. PERIOD. KISS KISS. PERIOD."

It's no surprise that in March 2020, at the beginning of the pandemic, WhatsApp saw a 40% jump in usage. Even my aunt, a lifelong Luddite who once had to be persuaded to even get a phone, decided to acquiesce in the absence of other options during the lockdowns. Though this seemed decidedly against the natural order of things, before we knew it we had established our own version of what now feels like a pillar of modern family life: the WhatsApp group.

Most people have found these virtual recreations to be a great source of comfort in these trying times. Certainly, the mundanity of everyday chitchat—photographs of my dad's endless jigsaws, my cousins' cats, even toddler toilet talk—has taken on emotional significance, mimicking the dynamics and tone of our real-life reunions. I remember the comfort I took as a child, for example, half-listening to my aunts murmuring about things like ancestors or hats or seersucker, like a radio providing background noise. The same can be said for a family WhatsApp group: Even if you're not paying attention, it's comfort enough just by virtue of being there.

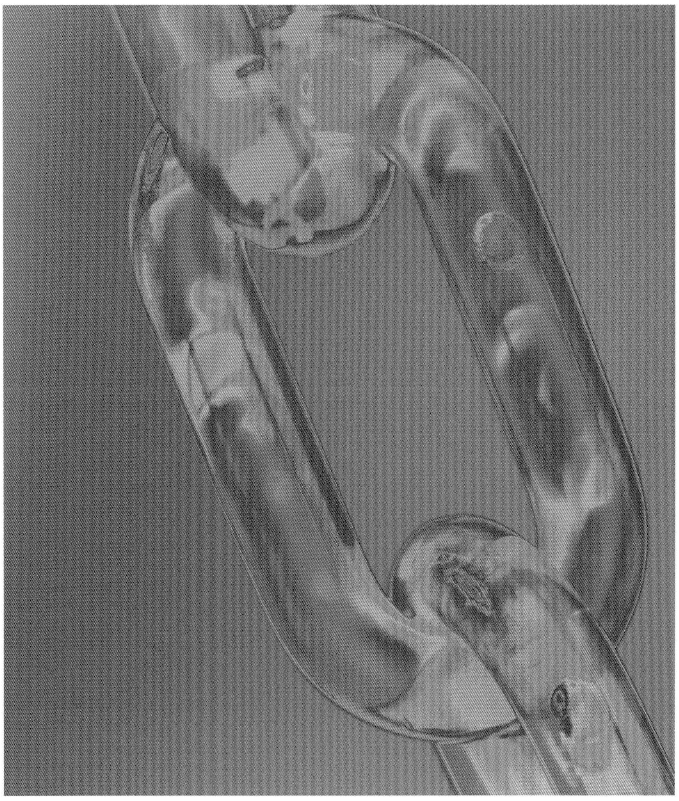

Yet for all the camaraderie, navigating the complexities of family relationships and intergenerational differences over subjects like, say, politics can still be as loaded on-screen as at the dinner table. A friend described descending into an explosive row with her sister. "There is no room for subtlety or nuance in WhatsApp. What could have been a conversation, or even a lively debate, turned into a virtual slanging match immediately."

Whatever your own experience, spare a thought for those who are struggling to even get the basics right. Earlier in 2021, Twitter was ablaze with a story about one family WhatsApp group, whose creator took his father, Peter, to task about never responding to any messages. It transpired he had actually added a plumber named Peter who had fixed his washing machine in 2013 and who had sat in the group silently for six months.

PT. 4
THE INTER NET.

Photography
GUSTAV ALMESTÅL
Set Design
ANDREAS FRIENHOLT

4.1 Elizabeth Douglas

(INTERVIEW)

Words STEPHANIE D'ARC TAYLOR

The wikiHow CEO upholding internet ethics.

WikiHow is the world's online user manual, featuring 100,000 how-to guides in English and another 300,000 in 18 other languages. There is an illustrated step-by-step for almost every social situation imaginable, including how to kiss someone, make friends and survive an ostrich attack. Even when you're looking up something embarrassing or unpleasant—like how to find deleted texts on your partner's phone—you're in a kind, judgment-free environment. That's intentional, says wikiHow CEO Elizabeth Douglas, and it reflects the ethos she and her team have built over the past 13 years.

STEPHANIE D'ARC TAYLOR: WikiHow has the reputation of being the nicest place on the internet. Have you nurtured this reputation intentionally?

ELIZABETH DOUGLAS: WikiHow was founded when Wikipedia was taking off and the idea of online collaboration was becoming a thing. In the beginning, we were really involved with the volunteer community and that set the tone for friendliness and helping people. What you're seeing [on wikiHow] is the product of a group of nice people that are passionate about helping. People ask me why I've worked here for so long; it's been 13 years, which is very uncommon in Silicon Valley. I can't imagine working somewhere else. I don't think that in any other job I would have such a big impact on the world.

SDT: WikiHow has endured some gentle mockery in pop culture. Is your team able to laugh along?

ED: Oh my gosh, yes. We're not so serious about it that we don't enjoy the pop culture things, the memes. We totally laugh at them; we think it's flattering. We actually just launched a wikiHow meme game—we've taken a bunch of our images out of context and created a game out of it.

SDT: WikiHow is very clearly a values-driven organization. Do you think it's an heir to the values of the early internet pioneers?

ED: We were founded during a time when people were literally just putting web pages up on the internet and trying to help people. Our business practices and operations and team have changed a lot during the years, but our values have stayed constant. Maybe it's the fact that we've been around so long that our approach is different than a company founded today.

SDT: What's the value of maintaining some of these early internet philosophies?

ED: We believe that people are empowered through education. WikiHow is translated into 18 different languages in addition to English. In English, wikiHow is maybe one of 10 or 100 articles on a topic; in another language, we might be the only article. If someone was searching the internet and didn't find our article, they might not be empowered to help themselves or solve their problem. I think of it as a really good friend, a really knowledgeable friend. What's neat about wikiHow is that it's always there for you, day or night, without judgment, as a friend would be. But it's knowledgeable about more topics than any one human being ever could be.

SDT: What's the most niche how-to you've seen on the site?

ED: How to survive in federal prison! It's been viewed 1.434 million times. Another article that's been really popular is how to survive an encounter with an ostrich.

SDT: What's the last thing you looked up on wikiHow for instruction?

ED: I use wikiHow all the time! I know our editorial process and I trust wikiHow a lot more than I trust many other sites on the internet. Most recently, I looked up how to cool yourself off without air conditioning—there was something about using fans with ice! I thought that was clever.

4.2
Yuri Arcurs

(INTERVIEW)

On the unseen art of stock photography.

As the self-proclaimed world's number one stock photographer, Yuri Arcurs shoots a surprising number of photos of people looking joyfully at their laptops while dressed in business casual. But the job entails a lot more than that: His Cape Town–based team of 100 also thinks deeply about the future, and what images people will need to represent it.

STEPHANIE D'ARC TAYLOR: How did you get started as a stock photographer?

YURI ARCURS: I got started on Shutterstock in around 2005. I was a psychology student and I went about photography like an academic exercise—looking at repeat purchases, customer tendencies, and making all kinds of statistics on what made an image sell. My sales completely took off. I made $10,000 per month over the next three months just by doing that exercise. I was customer-focused at a time when people were more artistically oriented.

SDT: How does the business of stock photography reflect current events?

YA: Our job is to be at the forefront of whatever is in demand. Our photos are not going to sell otherwise. That also means we shoot things that haven't happened yet. We've dealt with the pandemic in a couple of ways. We were ahead of the game in terms of the images that governments needed for the vaccine rollout; we had started shooting before there was a vaccine. Also, the trend of working from home: We shot a lot of "feeding your kids and working at the same time," but also dealing with stress and being tired, alcoholism, even using drugs at home. We shot images around political agendas, vaccine hesitancy and anti-COVID lockdown demos. We did a shoot with 30 people with signs—it looked very convincing!

SDT: So, is part of your job imagining dystopian futures?

YA: Right now, we're working on images around a potential China conflict. It's a gamble, but I don't think it's so much of a gamble as people think. We're far-out in terms of imagining the future: We're also doing space and aliens, UFOs, some funky stuff! We have to provide images that go the distance in terms of what an article needs.

SDT: What's the secret recipe for a good stock photograph?

YA: I can't answer that in a sentence! I can tell you that the most important thing is to get to the point, in terms of the concept of an image. You have to eliminate a lot of noise. The first step would be to clear up the junk that is confusing so that the message gets portrayed as clearly as possible.

SDT: What's the story behind your highest-selling image?

YA: Our top-selling shots aren't particularly interesting. Often, it's just a person with a laptop. Top-selling images aren't fun, but top-selling models are. They have to be generic, and look like they come from anywhere in the world. Our top-selling male model is a Brazilian man, but he looks a little Italian, maybe a little Indian. Handsome, but not that handsome. Too handsome [and he] can't be the dad or the good boyfriend.

SDT: Stock photographs are not generally considered for their artistic merit. What insight can you give to dispel that?

YA: That's a complete nonsense statement. That would have been true 10 years ago, but the level of the best stock photographers out there today is way higher than the commercial level. Because you can now make a living from it, some geniuses have popped up. I'm willing to challenge most established photographers against stock photographers. They wouldn't stand a chance.

Words
STEPHANIE D'ARC TAYLOR

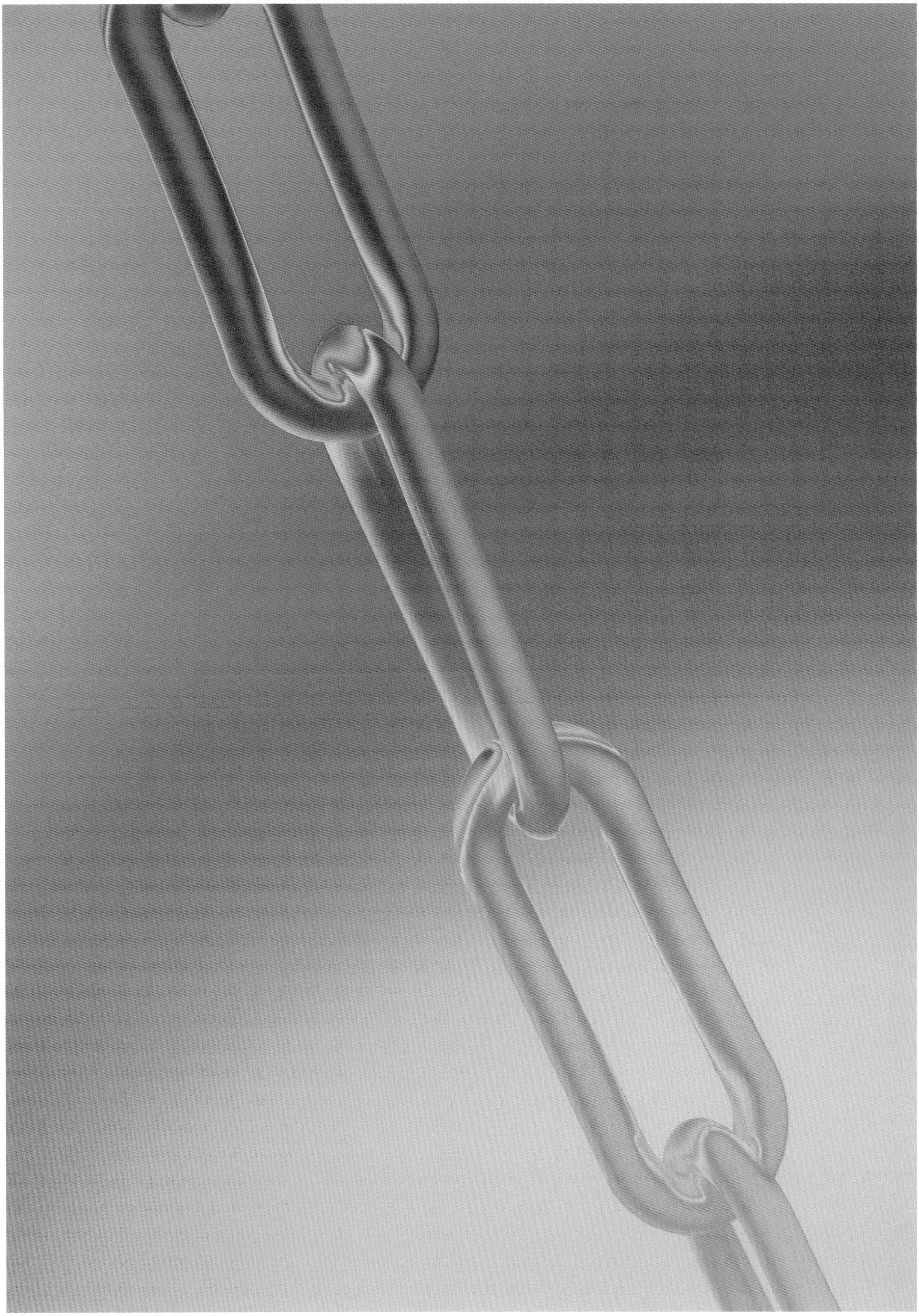

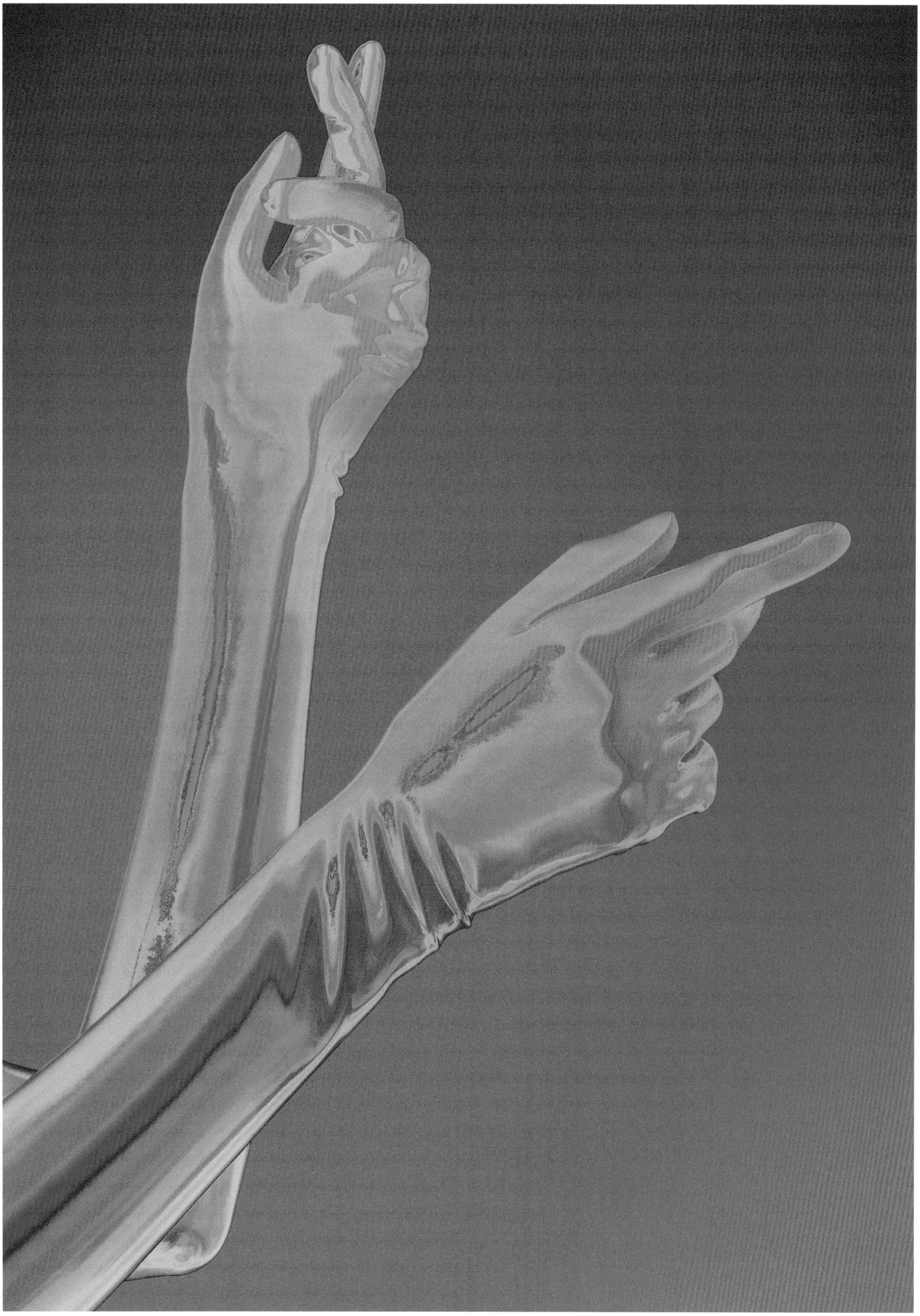

4.3

Remember the Internet

(INTERVIEW)

Meet the publishers archiving digital ephemera in print.

Words
NATHAN MA

On the internet, a moment might last a minute or a lifetime. To try to document its endless, ever-changing and increasingly hyperindividualized landscape inspires more questions than answers: Where would you start, and how? For Jeanne Thornton and Miracle Jones, the task begins close to home. As co-publishers of *Remember the Internet*, a series of books by Instar Books, the pair works with authors on putting out deeply personal accounts of bygone internet communities, exploring how these moments shaped not only online culture, but ourselves as individuals.

NATHAN MA: Recording the internet in print seems almost futile. What's at stake with this kind of archive-making?

JEANNE THORNTON: The whole idea of ephemerality is that it really does disappear. Technology, or the stylings of technology in its physical forms, changes so rapidly. But it's weird to think about how these changes play out in nonphysical technology, and particularly in environments online. The internet is a place to hang out. Unless you construct oral histories—particularly of things from the '90s and early 2000s that have already started fading from memory—there just won't be any record.

NM: How does the *Remember the Internet* series approach that ephemerality?

MIRACLE JONES: On the internet, there's a sense that there's no need to do history or to process things, because it's all going to be there. I think that's just totally wrong. It feels like a monolith—the internet is just one giant mass, like a wad of disgusting gum that we haven't thought about critically in the way that we have with other time periods. We're looking for anybody who is willing to do that work, which is horrible but hopefully fun.

JT: I think the strongest books are the ones where people come to us fascinated with a subject; they're personally haunted by it. People have intense relationships with the internet, and so you either have to have a really intense journalistic passion for it or a really intense personal passion. Both were the case with the first book in the series, *Tumblr Porn* by Ana Valens, which is a coming-of-age memoir of transness and erotic awakening through the internet, as well as a well-researched history of Tumblr down to the server-architecture level.

NM: Which online communities have shaped your own lives?

JT: The moment I knew I loved the internet was when I was 13; I was on AOL, searching for the comic *Calvin and Hobbes* and found this whole community of gamemakers who were making crude, unlicensed games. I realized that kids like me could make games and share them with one another. The games could be filthy, strange, mystical—they could be anything you wanted them to be. There was a feeling of vertiginous power. Now I realize how much of my life is spun from that time. My current day job came from someone who I met through a mutual friend from AOL in 1996.

NM: Have we lost that sense of connection on Web 2.0?

MJ: There's amazing stuff on Web 2.0, but there's also just massive amounts of money to be made. People focus on the entrails of Elon Musk or Jeff Bezos to determine the future, but the future is really in these side projects that no one's cottoned onto; projects that are beautiful, and what the kids will be doing next.

4.4
Brewster Kahle

(INTERVIEW)

The tech idealist archiving the internet.

As an idealistic technologist studying at MIT in the '80s, Brewster Kahle was enthralled by the possibilities the internet offered. In 1996, he established the Internet Archive, which he hoped would become "the Library of Alexandria for the digital age." Today, this free digital resource is used by 1.5 million people daily for its vast, crowdsourced collections of books, live concerts, television shows, software programs and audio recordings. Its most popular project, the Wayback Machine, allows anyone to access its archive of over 600 billion web pages that would otherwise have disappeared into the ether. Here, Kahle explains the human effort that goes into running a digital behemoth.

Words
PIP USHER

PIP USHER: How do you collect content for the Internet Archive?

BREWSTER KAHLE: There are now 800 different organizations—mostly libraries, universities, museums, historical societies—that participate by giving us lists of URLS and how frequently they should be archived. If they're interested in South American political elections, or their own institutional things, or zines, then we'll make those into their collections. They can download them and add them to their digital holdings, which we encourage because lots of copies keeps things safe. But we also have general robots that run around and try to collect as much as we can from homepages and then go down as deeply as we can.

PU: What have you archived recently?

BK: One thing that's been interesting are 78 rpm records, which came before vinyl. We've been digitizing all the ones we can find—all 287,078 rpm records. These are things you've never heard: yodeling, people whistling, accordions, Yiddish.

PU: Does some content on the internet have the right to be forgotten?

BK: Not all of the web was designed for the ages. It could be a painful time in your life that you'd prefer not to be enduringly visible. People write to us and ask to be taken down and we almost always do. But with public figures or politicians there's other considerations.

PU: You're based in a former church in San Francisco. What's the setup?

BK: We've installed servers that hold 70 petabytes of data in the sanctuary's great room. It's really hard to get a sense of how big this is from a data perspective, but physically it's kind of manageable. We've tried to make physical what for many people is purely virtual. Having people experience the internet by being able to see it—and even touch servers—is really important. We have Friday lunches where people come over and we introduce ourselves and say what we're up to. We're trying to lead an open life.

PU: How have you seen the internet change?

BK: Twenty years ago, we were running toward a world based on open-source materials. Now if you want to be heard you have to plug into Facebook or get published in someone else's magazine. The rise of the multinationals means we have fewer and fewer major corporations buying up all the magazines, all the scholarly journals and book publishers. We're seeing the world through screens, but what's on those screens is controlled by very few players globally. The heroes of the internet are its people. Hundreds of millions, or billions, of people are participating in the Internet Archive's radical experiment in sharing. The participation and the trust that people have put toward adding in what they know to the World Wide Web is fabulous.

PU: How might future generations use the Internet Archive?

BK: I hope it's displayed in a completely new and different way. What if you could walk into the library and talk to Albert Einstein and he answers in his tone of voice based on his writings? Or what if you could play the music that your parents had at their prom? Let's do something fun with all this.

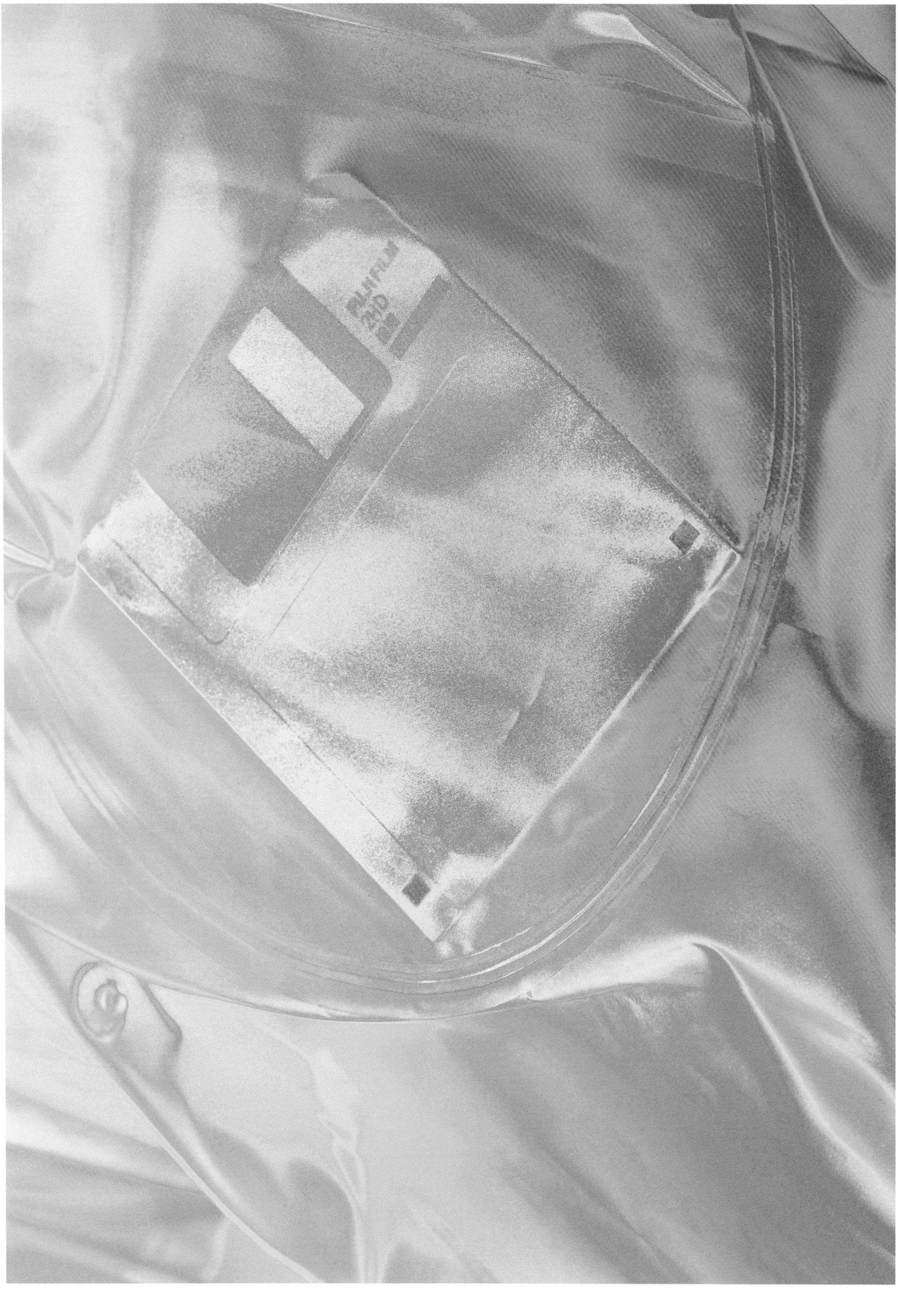
FUJIFILM
2HD

PT. 5
THE ATTENTION ECONOMY.

We invited Instagram content creators to answer a short survey about the influencer industry. Their anonymous answers offer an honest insight into the good, bad and downright ridiculous aspects of living life for the 'gram.

5.0

Influencers Anonymous

(Q&A)

Q.

Do you remember the moment you started addressing a public audience online?

The first time I was "recognized" in a public place was a real turning point. This person approached me and wanted a picture and to tell me why she followed me. I realized then that my followers weren't just a number but were actual people who cared about what I had to say.

I don't remember it entirely because I never aimed to have so many followers. The original intent was just to find a creative outlet and community online. I can't remember the exact moment everything shifted.

Back when Instagram was just starting out, the algorithm favored small accounts. I remember posting an image that went viral, which attracted a whole new audience. At that point, I knew I had something.

At first, I wanted to share my passion for fashion, style and travel. But a big push was losing friends who didn't understand me. I had no one to talk to, so I turned to the online family.

I started after I was on Season 8 of *American Idol*. I was sort of thrown into the deep end of living life publicly and I haven't looked back.

Words
HARRIET FITCH LITTLE

Q.

What advice would you give to someone who is thinking of turning their account public?

Remember, the moment you turn your account public, you're opening the gates for *everyone* to enter into your online world. You need to be okay with being judged and criticized.

Do it from a place of enjoyment. It's not very easy to grow an account on Instagram, so it has to be fun—particularly in the early stages when not that many people are coming along.

Think about your motivations and what you'd like to achieve with your public platform—it'll help you stay focused on what you're choosing to share.

It's important to be careful about what you say and to realize that, by being public, you can open yourself up to a lot of criticism. Many people are not able to handle that.

Turning your account public doesn't suddenly make you an influencer. There is a lot of work involved in building your voice and your audience. I don't know how many people have told me "it's so easy" to just take pictures and post them online. None of those people are still on Instagram.

I think it's best to do this for fun for a while before trying to have a career as a content creator.

Do it. Now is the first time in the history of *ever* where you can connect with humans around the world on an intimate and widespread level. It is more real than ever to make a living as an artist, as a creative and as an entrepreneur because of the connections that are possible. *Do not sleep on this opportunity!*

Q.

Is there anything that you wouldn't share on social media, or that you regret sharing?

It's probably the other way around. I wish I was able to share more of myself online, but I find it very difficult to do so.

I don't share our birthdates or where the kids go to school or when I'm on holiday. I'm quite anxious about the security aspect.

From experience, I know that when you start putting your relationship online and sharing more of you and your partner, you're opening your relationship up to judgment and this puts pressure on the both of you to live up to your audience's expectations. At that point, it starts to become less about you—especially once brand deals start flowing in trying to monetize your relationship.

I pretty much share everything. I have cried. I have talked about my sex life. I have shared about childbirth and breastfeeding and about my poops. I haven't talked about masturbation. . . yet. The day is young!

I regret casually saying I hadn't found a natural deodorant that worked and getting *hundreds* of DMs with suggestions. I try to only share things I want to talk about, otherwise, I get caught talking in my DMs about things I don't really want to talk about.

Q.

What's the most time-consuming and/or mundane aspect of being a content creator on Instagram?

The most time-consuming is responding to comments and DMs. The most mundane is filling out and reading through contracts.

Definitely the admin work. People never know what goes on behind closed doors, whether that's signing contracts or finding locations to shoot. A lot of work goes into being a content creator.

Lugging around tons of stuff and extra outfit changes. It's not glamorous and it's a lot more work than it looks!

Commenting back to people who ask where things you've tagged are from. Especially when there are no "pleases" or anything.

Community management. From engaging with new accounts to responding to countless direct messages, comments, etc., it can get exhausting. After a while, you start to realize that you're constantly consuming and not conserving any energy for yourself to focus on the actual creative aspect of being a content creator.

The app itself is the most time-consuming. And I guess that's the whole idea with Instagram, for us to just keep scrolling on a daily basis.

Q.

How has influencing changed your self-perception?

I've definitely become more self-confident, more sure of myself. I'm a much better public speaker than I used to be!

My voice has been lifted up on social media and on mainstream media in newspapers and documentaries, and that's allowed me to see that myself and other celebrities are not very different.

I'm more in tune with all aesthetic elements of my style and self, which is probably not a great thing. I have to edit so many pictures of myself that it's hard to not be aware of everything.

Honestly, it has definitely made me feel more negatively about myself. I am now constantly comparing myself to others and it's very difficult to stop. I don't feel as creative or innovative as I used to.

It's made me not care as much, because not everything you see online is real.

It's made me doubt myself. Made me cry. Made me giddy. But overall, it's made me feel more confident and empowered to be myself.

It undoubtedly took a toll on my mental health and self-esteem. I went down a rabbit hole of comparing myself with others which increased my anxiety levels. Setting boundaries for yourself is so important.

It has 100% made me more introspective and accountable. I've found that if I share my doubts, my fears, the shit that scares me, it shatters the belief that I am alone in those feelings. Public vulnerability is terrifying but also exhilarating.

It has strengthened my perception of reality. What I'm showing on Instagram is just a glimpse of my life or work or something I stage because the color, shape or whatever fits into my feed at that time. I try to see Instagram as a filter.

"I would walk a thousand miles to get the perfect photo."

Q.

What are the greatest lengths you've gone to for good content?

As a full-time employee of corporate America, it's already hard enough. I'm basically working two jobs and operating on three or four hours of sleep sometimes. I've woken up at 3 a.m. to watch the sun rise, spent stupid money on a dress and called in sick to work a few times.

I often set up mock picnics in beautiful locations for a quick video or photo. This involves hiking or trekking to interesting places with backpacks full of cameras, blankets and snacks.

Wow, this might be a little mean but. . . hanging out with fake content creators who used to use me for my ideas. I'm not sure why I was their friend for that long, but I guess I was a glutton for punishment.

I'd walk a thousand miles to get the perfect photo.

Bribery! I think I was so stressed about getting a photo once that I promised a Nintendo game in desperation!

Climbing on things, hanging off of things, driving to destinations, borrowing dogs, the list goes on and on.

I've traveled to various parts of the world to get good content. I've done trips solely to be inspired and create content. However, I began noticing that I was constantly exhausted and not enjoying my time on these trips. While it looked picture-perfect online, the realities behind the scenes were far from it.

I can't remember the exact number of countries I went through in one day, but it was something like five countries in 24 hours. A lot of the "trips" people see influencers going on are far from vacations, they are aggressive business trips to get great content efficiently. When family members go on business trips to exciting places, they tend to say they had a great time but didn't see the sights—they spent it in an office building, hotel or maybe a restaurant. Content trips can be similar, except instead of an office and hotel, it's all of the most photogenic sights. I've gone on a few vacations before where I didn't try to churn out content, and they were amazing.

A 4 a.m. hour-long hike up to Devil's Bridge in a wedding dress. That was fun!

I have created summer content swimming in the sea in February.

Re-filming a whole shoot five times as I thought the lighting was off (that took a whole week); walking the most dangerous plank walk in the world in China; running a marathon with no training; sitting with my feet dangling over a Hong Kong building. . . some stupid stuff, some dangerous and some just trying to create the cleanest and most perfect content. If a job's worth doing, it's worth doing right. . . right?

Q.

How do you feel about the phrase "cancel culture"?

I don't feel anything about it. It's there, it's happening, as it should—maybe. I tend not to be in any space where there's any negativity.

The idea of holding someone accountable for their actions is refreshing as long as they are given the space to grow from their mistakes.

I think social media has become such a powerful, very accessible way to gain information. Cancel culture is a product of this and influencers have a responsibility to make sure that the information they're sharing is accurate.

Many people say the wrong thing online and their careers are ruined for it without being given the chance to become educated or learn from their mistakes. Social media audiences are too quick to chastise someone over a bad comment because they can hide behind their handles.

I think it's very scary and although I think certain things should not be tolerated, I also believe in freedom of speech. It's good to stand up for what is right, but I don't think people should go out of their way to damage anyone's mental well-being.

It's a form of cyberbullying. We all have our flaws, and this culture is promoting an idea that a person is no better than the worst choice that they ever made.

It's important to stand up for what you believe, but yikes! I don't think I've met a single influencer that is not moderately terrified of saying the wrong thing or even the right thing the wrong way.

I feel I could get canceled just for stating my feelings about it.

Ugh. That's how I feel.

I don't know what it is!

PT. 6
THE ALGORI THM.

Photography
AARON TILLEY
Styling
SANDY SUFFIELD

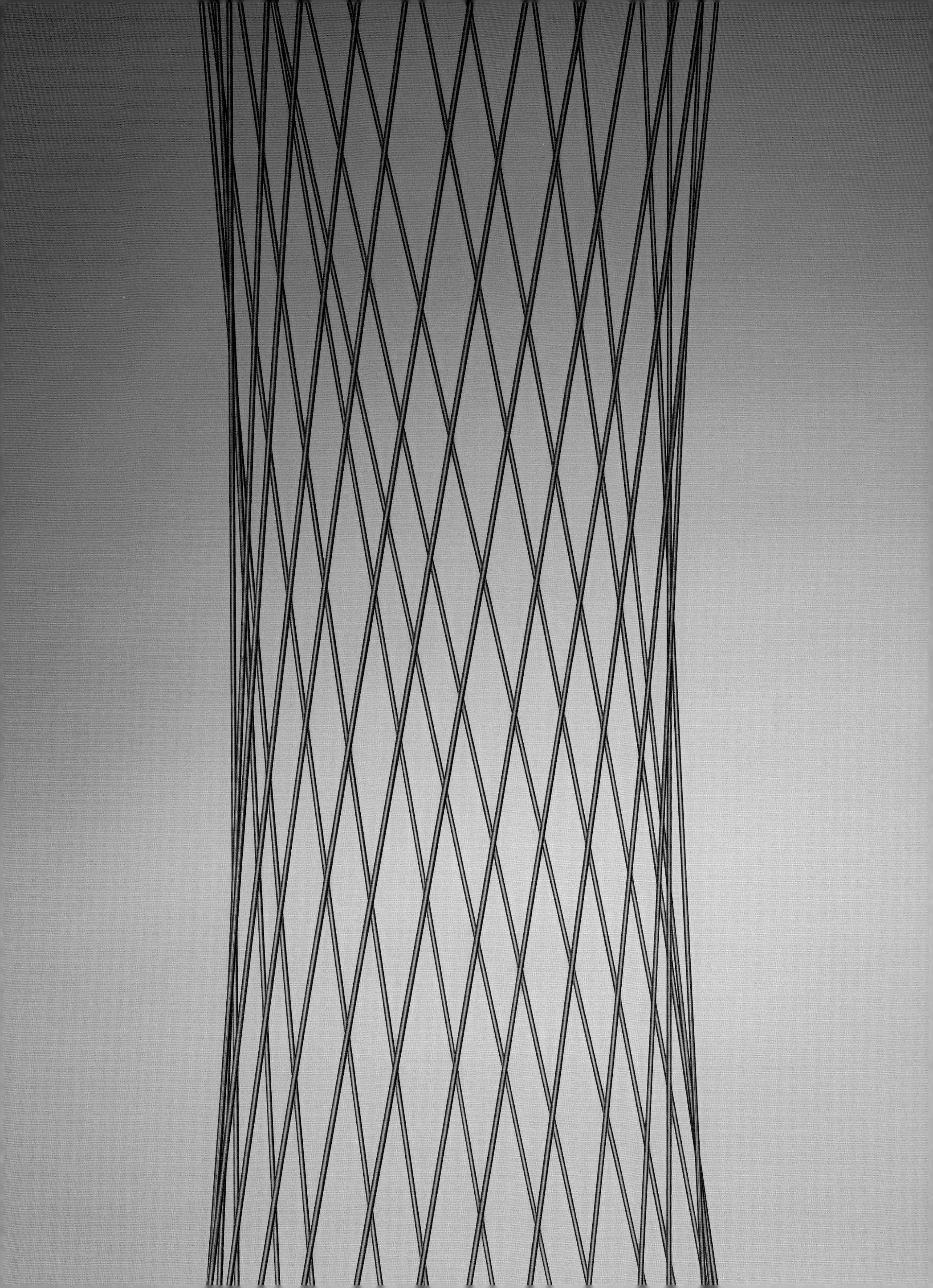

6.0

Rage Against the Machine

(ROUNDTABLE)

Today our lives are dictated by algorithms. They are used to determine credit ratings and hospital diagnoses, dating app matches and college admissions. Many of us have gotten used to robots making decisions about our lives, yet some remain understandably concerned. We most often come up against the whims of algorithms on social media, where they govern what content we see on our feeds and who sees our own posts. Recently, some content creators became enraged at a change to Instagram's algorithm which they claim has threatened their livelihood. We spoke to two experts about the ethics of Instagram's algorithm and the issue of forcing huge tech platforms to actually care about their users.

TOM FABER: Can you give me an introduction to how your work relates to social media algorithms?

CAROLINA ARE: I'm an online moderation researcher at City, University of London. I have a PhD studying online abuse and conspiracy theories, but lately my work has focused on algorithmic bias and moderation of nudity by social media platforms, partly stemming from my experience as a pole dance instructor and performer.

Words
TOM FABER

A conversation about the influence of invisible algorithms.

NICOLAS KAYSER-BRIL: I'm a journalist for AlgorithmWatch, an NGO based in Berlin which does advocacy and research around algorithms. I conducted a project for two years about Instagram's news feed algorithms which was shut down following pressure from Facebook.

TF: The algorithm can feel like a boogeyman in contemporary culture because it rules our digital lives and yet we don't understand it. Why were algorithms first introduced on social media?

NKB: The Instagram news feed algorithm replaced the chronological feed in 2016, with [Instagram owner] Facebook saying they wanted to optimize the experience so people wouldn't be flooded with content if they follow too many accounts. That's the official reason. The other perspective is that Facebook is optimizing for its own goal: revenue. The timeline algorithm tries to put users in a mood that will please advertisers.

TF: What content does the Instagram algorithm tend to prioritize or demote?

NKB: We conducted three projects before Facebook forced us to shut down our research setup by threatening legal action. Before that we'd noticed that posts using text were deprioritized, but the biggest takeaway was simply realizing how difficult it is to understand how the algorithms work. They're a black box and they're changing all the time. This makes platforms very difficult to investigate.

CA: At the moment, platforms aren't forced to be transparent. If my post is deleted, I'm told it's for "nudity and sexual activity," but not according to which standards. A woman showing cleavage might get her post taken down if she simply has bigger boobs than someone else. My account was deleted for nudity when the most recent picture was me, fully clothed, with my grandma. They told me it was a mistake, but the issue is that your content is being moderated yet you have no right to know why. These people are giving us nothing, essentially.

TF: Is there any justification in the companies keeping their algorithms so secret?

CA: It's business secrets; I think maybe they are afraid that people could exploit the system. But so much of public life happens on social media at the moment —look how algorithms promoted the attack on Congress, or demoted Black Lives Matter posts. It becomes worrying how little we know.

TF: Do you think users have a right to know how their posts are being filtered?

NKB: Citizens should be able to express themselves in public and today that usually means on social media. If you are to express yourself in an effective way, you need to understand how your voice will be spread. In the physical world that's obvious, but online it's impossible. So yes, people should be able to know how their voices are being shared online.

TF: AlgorithmWatch has shown that certain material, such as women in underwear, is prioritized by Instagram's algorithm in people's feeds. Yet Carolina has found that her pole dancing

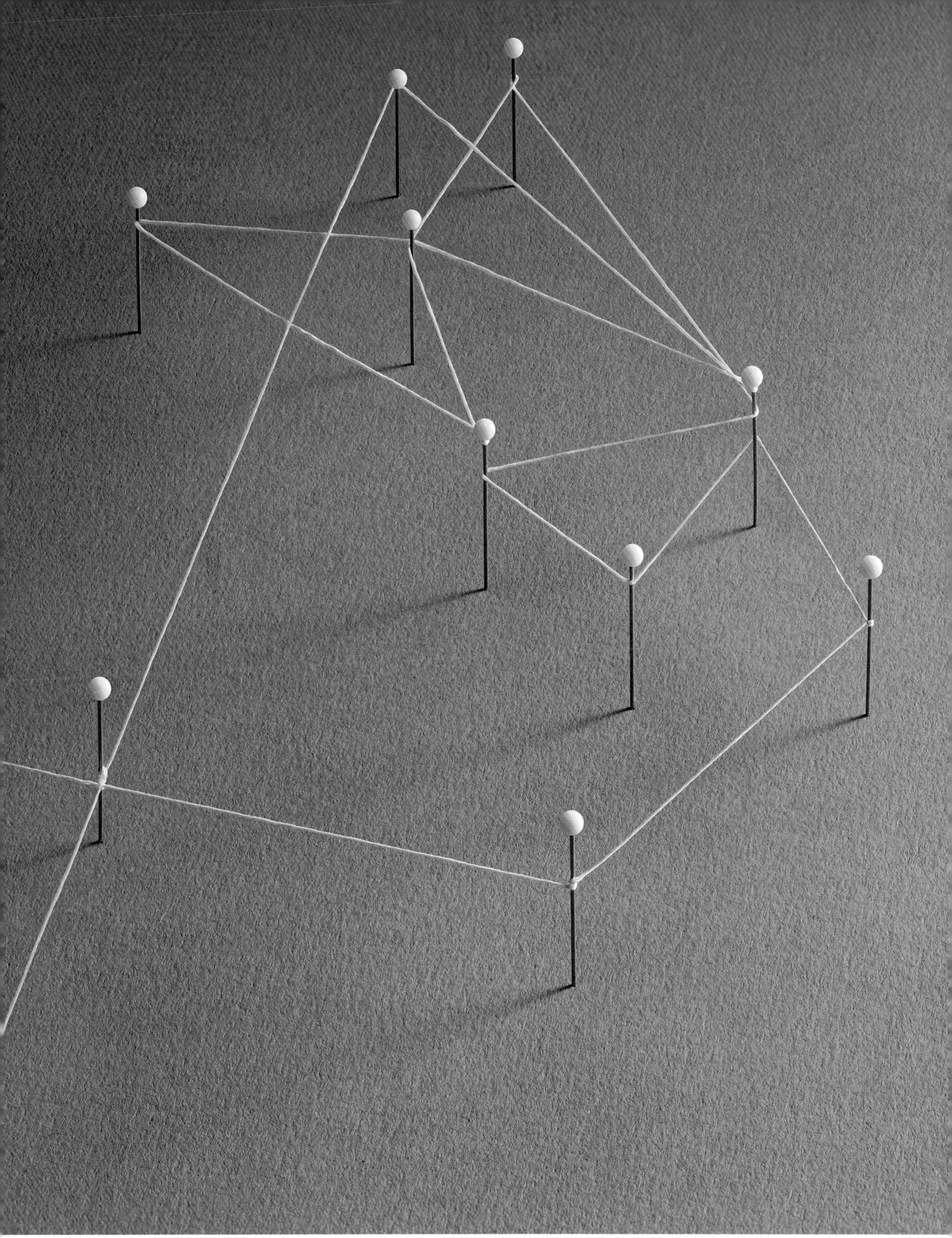

"Social media isn't just a civic space, it's also a marketplace."

content, which includes her dancing in similar clothing, has resulted in bans and warnings. How can we understand this contradiction?

CA: In a forthcoming paper I talk about the economic value of different bodies on Instagram. While pictures and videos of celebrities and models in bikinis are pushed to us on ads and our feeds, if it's the body of a plus-size user, LGBTQIA+ user, a person of color, a sex worker, or someone like me who performs an art created by sex workers, the moderation calculus changes. We are not a priority for platforms like Instagram, who apply very little nuance to their moderation. Sometimes I wonder whether there is an algorithmic binary that says: "Bikini + pole = no" but "bikini + model = fine."

TF: What specific recent changes in Instagram have upset users?

CA: It seems to be trying to maintain its power by basically mimicking TikTok with the new videos—"Reels"—which are promoted heavily but require much more labor to create. Meanwhile, the algorithm has changed to make it harder for creators to get their content seen by audiences. Engagement is going down for big accounts. For example, if others can't see my content, it will be harder for me to get brand partnerships or earn money from teaching. Social media isn't just a civic space, it's also a marketplace, and if you're making your money there, it's really damaging not to be able to reach audiences.

TF: Do you think that every change made to the algorithms is commercially motivated, and not done for the well-being of users?

NKB: Absolutely. These are private companies that only answer to themselves. They're optimized for their shareholders, not for society.

CA: So many lives and livelihoods depend on social media, yet these companies are still making commercially focused decisions. It's striking that platforms put such emphasis on the safety of their users but they also deprive users of that safety by deplatforming and censoring them. I'm sure nobody at Facebook wakes up in the morning with an evil plot to target creators and make their lives hard, but this is what their actions are doing.

TF: Some users say that their posts are not deleted but instead "shadow banned," meaning they aren't promoted on other people's feeds. Other users might not even know this is happening to them. Is this a reasonable way to moderate content?

CA: I don't think it's reasonable at all. If they decide something is a risk, it should be taken down. If it's borderline okay then it should stay up, rather than simply being demoted. It's a very opaque mechanism—a light form of censorship that they manage to get away with.

TF: Would it be sensible for creators to diversify rather than tying themselves to just one platform?

CA: Definitely. You can't tie yourself to one platform. Many creators are using their own websites, but beyond that we also need unions, charters of creators' rights and fairer work for moderators, too. We need a complete overhaul of the system of social media.

TF: Failing that, will creators keep serving the fickle algorithm indefinitely? Or will they eventually just leave?

CA: Social media is almost like an abusive relationship—platforms say they want you, but not that much, and you need to behave in a certain way. It's very confusing, and users always find themselves going back because these are the big platforms to be on. For me, I hate TikTok's moderation but I have 300,000 followers there, so it makes money for me. I can't afford to just drop it, even though it's exhausting and frustrating.

TF: Are recommendation algorithms like TikTok's even that effective?

NKB: Perhaps not. An interesting phenomenon is the Barnum effect, which says that when someone tells you that something has been made specifically for you, you tend to accept that fact, even if it's not true. Perhaps recommendation engines don't work that well after all, or maybe our interests evolve based on what we're given; so rather than simply predicting what we want, the algorithms are actually changing what we want to consume. But that hypothesis needs more research.

TF: How might things get better?

NKB: We need to show platforms that their algorithms are harmful and may not even be that effective. That they could work without them, or with simpler, more transparent algorithms. But the problem ultimately isn't the algorithms themselves, it's the structure of these companies in their quasi-monopoly position, and they won't change voluntarily anytime soon. The answer is in the political arena. Governments are the ones who allowed these platforms to grow to this enormous scale in the first place, so they need to take responsibility and create an incentive to produce fairer algorithms. Politicians and regulators have to create sensible legislation and agencies to enforce it.

TF: Does all this make you question why we use social media in the first place?

NKB: Sometimes, but that's a shame. We must bear in mind how transformative social media has been for communities that were previously totally absent from the media landscape. So there is a need for social media, we just need to shape it in a way that is still profitable to the companies that make it but less detrimental to our mental health.

(left) AlgorithmWatch's study followed a set of users who earn an income on Instagram to see if the algorithm favors certain types of content over others.

PT. 7
ARTIFICIAL INTELLIGENCE.

7.1

Computed Emotion

(ESSAY)

On the rise of chatbot therapy.

Words RACHEL CONNOLLY

What do you think of when you hear a phrase like "mental health chatbot" or "virtual therapy assistant"? Do you imagine a glitchy interface, robotic questions and a sterile textbox format in which to document your most private thoughts and feelings? Perhaps you picture an easy, cheap way to keep on top of your mental well-being; something less intimidating than starting therapy with a person. It's possible your mind turns immediately to privacy and data leaks. Or maybe you think simply of an app you're already using.

It's hard to quantify exactly how many people use mental wellness apps, partly because there are so many different options available. According to the American Psychiatric Association, there are around 20,000 such apps on the market. But the number of subscribers is certainly substantial—the most popular of these have tens of millions of users (Headspace, for example, has 60 million, while the Replika chatbot has around 7 million).[1]

Whatever your opinion, there are no wrong answers here. Much like feelings about therapy in general, attitudes to app-based mental health services are personal.

Even if you have not interacted with a chatbot in a mental health context, you may well have done so in a customer service setting. These programs engage users in a dynamic conversation: They generally allow you to type a question, or select a statement from a suggested list, and then they generate an appropriate response. Lots of companies have incorporated this technology into their complaints and booking procedures. In a mental health context, the questions and communication style (the "voice" that the chatbot uses) are different, but the premise is the same.

Some see these apps as part of the solution to the serious problem of lack of access to mental health support in a clinical setting. According to the advocacy group Mental Health America, almost 60% of those with a mental illness of some kind last year had no treatment. Siobhan McDonold, the clinical director of digital psychiatry for Beth Israel Deaconess Medical Center in Boston, tells me that hybrid models, which combine therapy with an app to use alongside treatment can be successful. She explains, "[They] may help patients improve quicker, and ultimately allow providers to see more patients." Given the current mental health crisis in the US, she adds, "this can be a really great thing."

One of the touted advantages of therapy-style wellness apps (and a point made in much of the marketing around them) is that they are cheaper than in-person therapy. The national average cost of a 45-minute to 1-hour therapy session is $90 (it tends to range between $60 and $120, but can reach $250), meaning a month of weekly sessions can cost roughly $360. Meanwhile, many of the apps offered are currently free, thanks to venture capital funding. Another advantage is that they can be accessed anywhere, at any time. McDonold says they can also "help reduce any fear around stigma related to seeking mental health support." While therapy and certain mental health conditions (like depression and anxiety) are increasingly destigmatized among the professional classes in the US, this is not the case everywhere.

Shengying Xu, a 32-year-old based in Chicago who started using a popular app called Woebot last October, tells me that downloading the app seemed less intimidating than in-person therapy. "I grew up in China and the culture of thinking around therapy there is very different to America," she says. "The way I grew up, the thinking was that if someone is in therapy that's because something has gone really wrong." Based on a model of cognitive behavioral therapy (CBT), Woebot allows users to submit statements and it responds accordingly. It also offers exercises to help its users learn how to, say, manage anxious thought patterns.

Xu's experience with Woebot has been very positive. "It really turned my mental health around when I started using it," she says. "I still use it almost every day." Now, though, she views it more as an educational tool than as a therapist, and she sees it as a way of learning CBT interactively rather than through reading a textbook. Some of the dozen-odd app users I spoke to described similarly positive experiences. Others reported frustrations over clunky interfaces and the limitations of still very basic design features. (Even Woebot, which is one of the more advanced apps, does not allow users to type their own statements or questions; they must instead choose from a menu.)

(1) In April 2020, the FDA decided to suspend its usual rules around digital therapeutic devices for psychiatric disorders. Previously, only a handful of platforms had been approved, but the urgency of providing care remotely during the pandemic meant that doctors were suddenly allowed to prescribe several relatively new apps to patients.

Amelia Horgan, a 29-year-old academic researcher and author based in the UK, told me that as part of a course of CBT provided by the National Health Service, she had to use an app called ReachOut Worry Time, which instructs users to write down their worries on virtual slips of paper and swipe them into a virtual area to save them until "worry time." She found it frustratingly simplistic. "I can see that there are some people who might not have thought to try something like this on paper themselves before, but the fact that this is frontline for everyone below the level of immediately suicidal is mental," she says. In fact, the vast majority of the apps use CBT-style techniques and this style of treatment, like any, has variable results. And, while the premise of improving access to mental health care is one of the selling points, the vast majority of these apps cater to a limited range of conditions: anxiety, depression and autism in children.

But many people who can benefit from the apps have found the technology useful. Xu, for example, says she feels more comfortable communicating with a digital interface rather than starting a relationship with a therapist, particularly when she's feeling low. This point seemed to be divisive among the users I spoke to. While several agreed with Xu, others said they felt a kind of revulsion at the idea of communicating such personal information to an app. "It was so faceless. And the idea of writing out deeply personal feelings and thoughts into a faceless online void, which would be checked at some point and commented on, like a kind of fucked-up social media, was so off-putting," says Griff Ferris, a legal and policy officer in London, of his experiences with SilverCloud, another app used by the NHS.

Some people are more comfortable with the idea of communicating personal information with a computer than others. This was evidenced by the first ever chatbot, which was designed not to perform therapy, but to demonstrate that "communication between man and machine was superficial." In the mid-1960s, a computer scientist at MIT named Joseph Weizenbaum wrote a program called ELIZA. It was programmed to accept statements from a client and respond by reframing these statements as questions, or empathetic statements, thereby parodying Rogerian therapy, a client-centered therapy. A Rogerian chatbot is comparatively easy to program because it does not need to analyze the language used by the "patient" to choose a suitable response; instead, it reframes whatever the user has said as a question or a statement. A statement such as "I hate my father," for example, might elicit the generic response "Why do you hate your father?"

The computer did not (and, of course, still does not) understand what the client was actually saying on any emotional level. But Weizenbaum was shocked to find that people still acted like patients when communicating with it. "I was startled to see how quickly and how very deeply people conversing with [ELIZA] became emotionally involved with the computer and how unequivocally they anthropomorphized it," he wrote in *Computer Power and Human Reason*.

There were other experiments in the 1960s and 1970s: A program called SHRINK, pioneered by Kenneth Colby—a psychiatrist and psychoanalyst at Stanford—was developed to be used for therapy. A chatbot named PARRY was programmed to communicate like a person with paranoid schizophrenia. And, in 1965, Warner V. Slack became the first person to put a patient in conversation with a program. But therapy (or therapy adjacent, at least) apps did not become widely used until recently. The recent uptake of mental health apps owes something to the ubiquity of mobile phones, advances in chatbot technology in other contexts, and perhaps to issues with accessing traditional therapy during the pandemic.

Hannah Zeavin, an academic at the University of California, Berkeley, charts the different forms of therapy mediated by technology, from early suicide hotlines to Zoom therapy, in her new book, *The Distance Cure: A History of Teletherapy*. She sees ELIZA, along with more recent chatbots, as examples of a sort of self-soothing that she terms "auto-intimacy." She tells me that while she sees these apps as distinct from the therapy process, what they offer is not as new as it might seem. She likens the service to diary keeping or even self-soothing habits, like sucking our thumbs as infants.

What is new though, as Zeavin points out, is the potential for privacy invasion. "These apps and tools have been rife with privacy problems, which totally upends the principle of confidentiality in a clinical setting," she says. Various studies surveying data collection practices across mental health apps have determined that many share data with other companies. A recent investigation by *Consumer Reports* found that several, for example, share data with Facebook. One of the selling points of these apps is that they can be less intimidating to a person who views therapy with suspicion but, as Zeavin says: "I worry about how devastating a leak would be, for someone who is so hesitant to even speak about their problems to another person. That's always the bottom line, for me."

Not many of the people I spoke to mentioned concerns over privacy, but at this point we are inured to the idea of companies collecting data about us. And for someone in a low place, it might seem like a theoretical concern only.[2]

This is not to say the apps are unhelpful—after all, plenty of the people I spoke to found them to be useful—but these questions about privacy and commercialization are worth exploring. In *The Distance Cure*, Zeavin defines the rise of these apps, often backed by Silicon Valley money, as the "corporate turn" for mental health mediated by technology. The promise of improved access and low-cost democratization sits uncomfortably alongside the fact that digital mental health has become a multibillion-dollar industry, according to an estimate by the American Psychiatric Association. Many of these apps are free, on the face of it, but at what cost?

(2) Data breaches aren't exclusively the concern of AI-based therapy companies. In October 2020, news broke that the largest provider of private psychotherapy care in Finland had experienced a cyberattack and the notes of 40,000 patients were accessed by hackers. The criminals went on to extort several patients and publish private records online.

7.2
Captcha This

(PHOTO ESSAY)

Select all squares with CACTUSES. If there are none, click skip.

Photography
ROMAINE LAPRADE

Select all squares with BOATS. If there are none, click skip.

Select all squares with MAN-MADE OBJECTS. If there are none, click skip.

Select all squares with AN EMPHEMERAL AURA OF OPTIMISM.
If there are none, click skip.

178 — 192

PEER REVIEW

Words:
Shirin Neshat

Iranian artist and filmmaker SHIRIN NESHAT pays homage to the iconic Egyptian singer OUM KULTHUM.

Oum Kulthum appeals to the activist in me. She was an unconventional woman who became the most important artist of the 20th century in the Middle East. Having risen in the male-dominated society of 1920s Egypt, she had a five-decade career and died beloved—a mythical figure. Her music's power in bringing people to truly primal emotions, like weeping, is unlike anything I've ever seen. She also broke through taboos—between men and women, the religious and the secular. In Israel, Algeria, Iran, there may have been fighting, but they agreed on Oum Kulthum.

My love for her grew from childhood. My parents listened to her music, but back then, it felt too classical. It was only in my 30s, when I was in the US, that I started paying attention. I don't understand Arabic, except in prayer, yet the extraordinary emotions of her music resonate deeply.

Once you have fallen under the spell of Oum Kulthum, you have fallen in love. I can only compare it to being drugged. I cannot tell you how many Arabs compare her to ecstasy—the experience of listening to her music transcends the reality of everyday life. You lose all sense of time and place.

I get choked up, and immediately feel a deep sense of melancholy, because I'm in the West. It reminds me of this disconnect. Maybe if I was in Egypt or Iran, I wouldn't feel it so much. I only wish that I could do what she did—leave behind a work or two that, when people look afterward, they would be so overwhelmed that they could cry.

Instead of having a traditional life, she devoted herself to her art. As a smaller artist looking up to her, I see my own conflict about following tradition.[1] Like her, I'm completely devoted to my art, yet I can't abandon my personal life—I've had a child. Oum Kulthum was very secretive about her private life. She kept her sexuality unknown. I'm uncomfortable about being in the public sphere—I understand there is a duty but my private, vulnerable self battles against it. I learned from her that, ultimately, the art is what's important. *As told to Bella Gladman*

(1) *Looking for Oum Kulthum* is a 2017 feature film directed by Shirin Neshat and Shoja Azari. It depicts a female artist exiled from Iran, trying to make a film about Egypt's most revered singer. Aspects of the narrative echo Neshat's own life: She was banned from reentering Iran, the country of her birth, in 1996. The "film within a film" format sidesteps the dearth of biographical detail available about Oum Kulthum, who famously refused to let journalists take notes or record her in interviews, calling tape recorders "pieces of iron." Neshat supplemented her research by visiting Kulthum's family in Cairo.

OBJECT MATTERS

Words:
Stephanie d'Arc Taylor

A modest history of the codpiece.

According to Cambridge academic Victoria Miller, the BBC's 2015 adaptation of Hilary Mantel's Henry VIII palace procedural *Wolf Hall* was not only "fantastic" but generally quite historically accurate—except for one, not-so-small omission. The codpieces, she told *The Guardian*, were "way too small to be accurate—they should be at least double the size."

Miller is a leading expert on the codpiece, a relatively flash-in-the-pan fashion trend that no chivalrous young gentleman in the early- and mid-16th century would have been caught dead without. Initially, incredibly, the codpiece—a pouch of structured fabric placed over the genitals—was designed to be a modesty garment as more revealing styles of hose and doublets came into vogue. But as the advent of chivalry required men to loudly herald their gallantry, the codpiece changed also, into an attention-grabbing showpiece.

By the end of the 16th century, the codpiece had fallen out of favor. Its decline was noted, and celebrated, by the French philosopher Michel de Montaigne, who in the 1580s observed that the garment was designed to draw attention to a part of the body that couldn't even be mentioned in polite society. "An empty and useless model of a member," he sniffed.

Four centuries later, the codpiece made a triumphant return—and not just in the men's locker room thanks to its sporty cousin, the jockstrap. Leather daddies began adopting it in the 1960s, and the style was later borrowed by heavy metal icons Judas Priest. In the late 1980s, Axl Rose toured wearing a leather codpiece and chaps, his lily-white inner thighs visible to all. Jean Paul Gaultier famously sent codpieces down the runway, most memorably paired with strappy beige corsets.

The codpiece is an exhibitionist's kiss-off to conventional fashion and morality. (Reportedly, the *Wolf Hall* codpieces were small because the American producers of the program were scandalized by their historically accurate size.) It's a far cry indeed from the time when no modest man was without one.

Photo: WBC ART / Alamy

Words:
George Upton

In the foothills of the Alps, socialism, modernism and manufacturing came together in IVREA, Olivetti's remarkable "company town."

For three decades, a small Italian town in the foothills of the Alps was the center for radical new ideas around industry and community. Ivrea, some 30 miles north of Turin, had been the headquarters of typewriter manufacturer Olivetti since the company was founded by Camillo Olivetti in 1908. Between 1933 and the late 1950s, under the dynamic new leadership of Camillo's son Adriano, the town was transformed into an experimental utopia, promising a humanized approach to the organization of labor.

Adriano believed passionately in the social responsibility of industry: Olivetti employees enjoyed benefits that were unparalleled in Italy, including flexible working hours, free childcare and access to affordable housing. A socialist with an interest in urban planning, Adriano expanded his father's small redbrick factory into a sprawling complex of glass and steel, hiring some of the greatest names in Italian modernist architecture to create light-filled workshops. To encourage employees to educate themselves, Olivetti built reading rooms and libraries and offered courses in culture and engineering. The canteen building was imagined by Ignazio Gardella as an oasis of calm, immersed in the natural landscape, while Luigi Figini and Gino Pollini's nursery was described by MoMA as the most distinguished building ever commissioned by a company.

Design had always played an important role in the company. The very first Olivetti typewriter, launched in 1911, was bold and simple with a careful color scheme—aesthetically appealing rather than mechanically innovative. Under Adriano, design came to be considered as important as technology or management, leading to products like the iconic Lettera 22, designed by Marcello Nizzoli and launched in 1950.[1] The modernist architecture that Adriano commissioned for his utopian company town had a similar focus,

where through function and beauty the factory was not only to be a place of production but the driving force behind the economic and social development of Ivrea. As Diane Ghirardo, a professor of architecture who writes about Italian modernism, explains, "He really believed in a notion of work where you could engage with the world, where you could grow and prosper."

Most people would have encountered Adriano's vision at the La Serra Complex, an imposing steel structure that was situated—unlike the company's factories and offices—at the edge of the cobbled, historic center of Ivrea. Comprising a hotel where Olivetti's international staff would stay when visiting the company's headquarters, and a cultural center that included a movie theater, auditorium and restaurant, the complex was open to all residents of Ivrea, not just employees. Though it was built after Adriano's death in 1960, the complex, designed by Iginio Cappai and Pietro Mainardis, is the most visible symbol of Olivetti's legacy in Ivrea.

Despite some early success in computing, Olivetti failed to keep pace with a changing industry and the company was eventually broken up. Today the La Serra Complex, like much of the Olivetti-built town, lies empty and unused. In 2018, UNESCO recognized Ivrea as a World Heritage site, and many rediscovered the town through a *New York Times* piece by Nikil Saval; the comments section of the article became a community forum for those who worked for Olivetti and for people who had visited the town. The bold, visionary architecture remains a ghostly monument to Adriano's utopia—a physical embodiment of the nostalgia shared by thousands in Ivrea and around the world for a fleeting moment of harmony between the demands of industry and the individual.

(1) The Lettera 22 was the typewriter of choice for Günter Grass, Joan Didion and William S. Burroughs. In 1959, the Illinois Institute of Technology named it as the best design product of the previous 100 years.

Photo: Nick Ballón

TORREY PETERS

Photo: Camila Falquez

Words:
Jenna Mahale

The *Detransition, Baby* author is living her best life.

Torrey Peters has never written with her detractors in mind, and she doesn't plan to start just because her debut novel, *Detransition, Baby*, is now a bestseller. "I think it's very important to not write defensively," she says, reflecting on how the book was at risk of being weaponized as a transphobic talking point. "I'm conscious about who I choose as my audience, but I'm not conscious about thinking of all the ways that bigots could twist my words."

In the novel, hot trans girl protagonist Reese has grown weary of the chaotic social life she leads and starts to consider entering a co-parenting setup with her ex, Ames, who has detransitioned after living as a trans woman and is now having a baby with a cis woman—also his boss—named Katrina. Peters' emotionally intelligent comedy of manners has won near-universal praise since its January release, landing a spot on the Women's Prize for Fiction longlist as well as a forthcoming Shondaland TV adaption. Now, the author splits her time between a secluded cabin in Vermont and her colorful Brooklyn apartment. She calls me from the latter when we speak—about truth in fiction, her future writing and fiddlehead ferns.

JENNA MAHALE: Have you always wanted to be a writer?

TORREY PETERS: In my adult life, I was. But I wasn't one of those kids who grew up being like, "I'm going to be a writer." What I have always been more of is a reader. And the writing was a natural outgrowth of how much time I spent reading. When I started college, I took a writing class for fun and found that I had internalized a lot of the rhythms of narrative without ever really studying it or reading it. And the idea of the sort of pleasure that reading had given me being something that I could offer to other people slowly grew.

JM: You've spoken about the importance of "telling hard truths" through fiction. Which authors or works do you look to for expertise in that sense?

TP: I think that Elena Ferrante's *Neapolitan* series hits that level of urgency, that level of ferocity. Eve Babitz did it in her first book in a delightful way. Thomas Bernhard, in how angry he was about art and Austria, wrote *Woodcutters* and *The Loser*—that was unbelievable truth telling, just so incredibly bracing.

JM: I read that you roast your own coffee. Do you have any other secret foodie habits?

TP: I've recently discovered that the KitchenAid stand mixer has a pasta attachment. If you make a big batch of dough—maybe two or three cups—you can make a personal-sized fresh pasta meal in the same amount of time it takes you to make a sandwich. Of course, you have to buy a KitchenAid stand mixer first. But for me, it's just the price of six dinners in an Italian restaurant over the course of my life.

JM: What's the best meal you've made yourself recently?

TP: I spend a lot of time in an off-grid cabin up in Vermont. We have no running water, and our electricity is solar so it can't run any appliances. So I've been learning meals that I can cook over one burner, oftentimes with just local ingredients. And the other week, I made a fiddlehead pizza. Fiddlehead ferns are so good. They taste sort of like asparagus, but fresher, I think.

JM: Do you see that retreat into nature as an important part of your writing process?

TP: It's provided a very balancing contrast to my life in Brooklyn in the last year or so. But [in terms of writing] it's more incidental. I'll spend two or three hours cutting or clearing trees; the whole time I'm thinking about projects that are in my head, but I'm not worrying about talking with agents or anything. So much of the writing process for me is about getting space, to let the insights sort of trickle in, and have your subconscious do work for you. The cabin is about letting my brain breathe so that when it's time to type, there's gas.

JM: The dedication in *Detransition, Baby* was to "divorced cis women"—who or what do you think your next novel will be an homage to?[1]

TP: I don't know right now, but by the time it's published I would like to be able to have a very pithy idea of who I want to read it, and then the audience can grow from there. [My next novel] has to do with money, and the ways that we relate to money in terms of identity, the ways that money offers access to power and how you can speak through and about identity in order to get access to power.

(1) Peters read the work of divorced cis women prior to writing her novel and noted the parallels between their experiences post-marriage and those of trans women: Both are obliged to start over again—to reassess who they are and be honest about how they want to live—at a point in life where identity is presumed to be well-established.

BAD IDEA: YEAR WRAPS

Words:
Ed Cumming

An algorithmic celebration of your most depressing digital data.

Blame Spotify. If you are one of its 355 million users, then you will likely know about the end-of-year "Wrapped" roundup. Each December, a jaunty video tells you which songs and artists you listened to most in the preceding 12 months. There's no hiding from the data. In your mind, you were listening to trap and experimental techno. In reality, you were listening to adult standards and help-me-sleep whale sounds. Still, if you want to advertise to the world that you are in the global top 1% of Phish fans, this list is your chance.

It's a neat idea, for Spotify. The problem is that anything that works in tech is immediately adopted by other companies. And what works for music does not work for every customer relationship. I like to order takeout as much as the next man, but do I need a summary reminding me that I've had 30 curries and 26 chicken burgers over the course of our last trip around the sun—plus, just once, ice cream in the morning? Or my banking app telling me how much I spent on "leisure"? Or Uber letting me know that I should really just divert my earnings directly to them,

Photo: Max Cavallari

rather than going through the charade of holding the money in my account?[1] Trainline, a UK-based travel booking site, was widely (and rightly) mocked when its 2020 roundup reminded users that it had been a tricky year for long-distance travel.

Where does it end, all this algorithmic nonsense? Can we look forward to cutesy notes from our healthcare providers telling us how much weight we've put on? Warnings from the municipality about the number of wine bottles in our recycling bin? These firms want to create an illusion of friendliness, a way to suggest to us that we are not merely another drop in an ocean of anonymous users. But tech firms succeed because they offer convenience. By design, they let you forget you are ordering takeout and getting cabs in the hope that you will do so more often. Nobody wants to stare their own human weakness in the face. There's enough of that around during the holidays anyway. And there's a fine line between a charming new algorithmic data tool and that most old-fashioned "end-of-year wrap-up": the credit card bill.

(1) Users of the trading app Robinhood, which markets itself toward a younger demographic than most brokerages, received slick slideshows recapping their "investing journey" for 2020. One user posted a screenshot showing he'd checked the value of his Tesla stock 18,656 times (more than 50 times a day).

GOOD IDEA: HONEST AI

Words: Harriet Fitch Little

Spotify's Year Wrapped feature launched earnest copycats, but also jokey parodies. Developers Mike Lacher and Matt Daniels at *The Pudding* went so far as to create a bot that mimics the sites' process and formula to mock users' musical proclivities. *How Bad Is Your Spotify* bases its algorithmic understanding of "good" music on the opinions of dogmatic sites such as *Pitchfork*, and judges a user's Spotify listens according to how far they deviate from it. It spits out creative insults such as "learns-about-rap-from-TikTok-bad" or "manic-pixie-dream-girl-bad" before slapping a final rating on your listening habits. The app is ultimately not as personalized as it appears to be, and the AI is not as sophisticated: It gives all users the same prompts and dishes out similar insults with the artists' names swapped in and out. But this is exactly the same mechanism Spotify uses to make users feel special. If a bot can be your cheerleader, it can be your cyberbully too.

BACK TO BASICS

Crossword: Mark Halpin

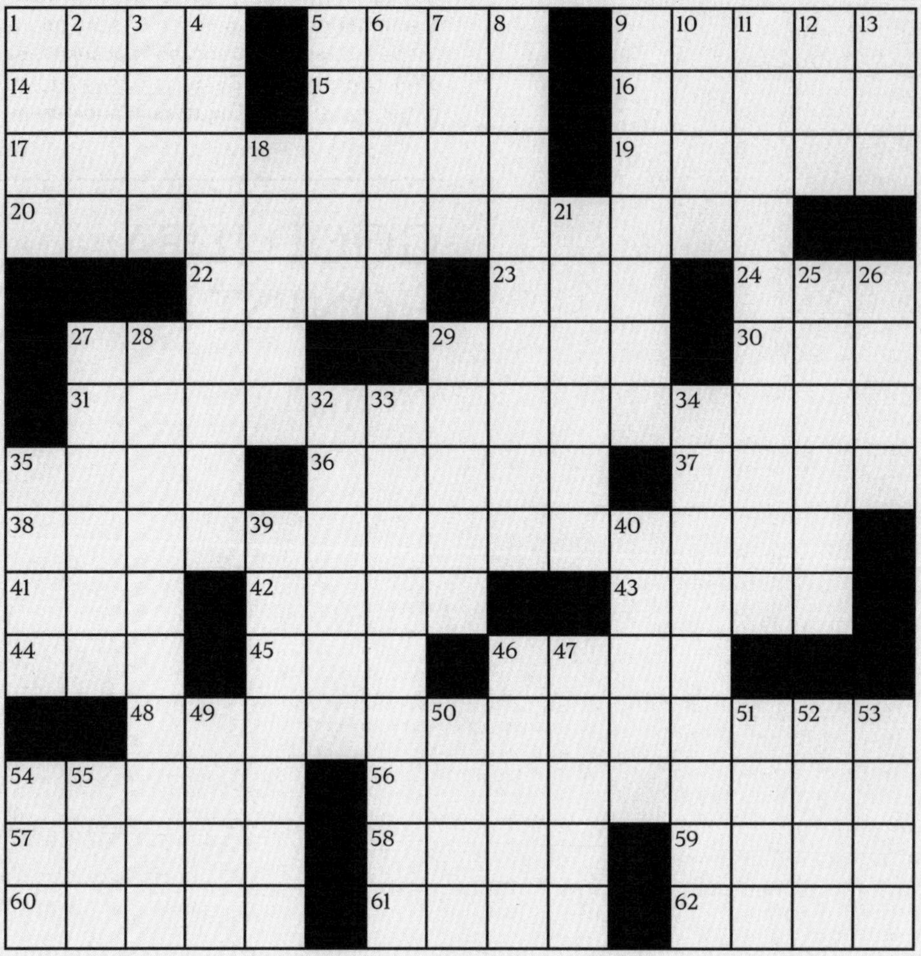

ACROSS

1. Magician's prop
5. Thomas Edison's middle name
9. Recipient of philanthropy, perhaps
14. Jazz legend Fitzgerald
15. One who regrets
16. *Gone with the Wind* role
17. Sucrose that doesn't come from cane
19. Ancient Peruvians
20. One who's devoutly convinced of the existence of a simple machine?
22. Drink at a Renaissance Faire
23. Vista, in Vichy
24. The Buckeyes of college basketball, in brief
27. Baseball great once engaged to J. Lo
29. *The Americans* actress Russell
30. Music genre or family member
31. Simple machine in a combination that might bring tears to your eyes?
35. A little, musically
36. Not very intuitive, perhaps
37. Potter's material
38. Replay of a simple machine's track event?
41. LGBT activist Savage
42. Yearly nos. calculated on a loan
43. E.g., the Smithsonian, for short
44. The Concorde, for one
45. A little square of butter
46. Dallas, Texas, to fans
48. Romantically inclined toward a simple machine (or two)?
54. Cheer for a prima donna
56. Renaissance sculptor or Ninja Turtle
57. Out of bed
58. Mao Tse-____

59. Got older
60. Eightsome
61. Guestimator's phrase
62. Classic movie comedienne West and namesakes

DOWN
1. Spider's homes
2. Knighted actor Guinness
3. Dodger or Met, for short
4. A romantic film might make a good one
5. Island in the Dutch Caribbean
6. Went downhill on a Winter Olympics team
7. Osso buco ingredient
8. Reached, as a conclusion
9. Apt venue for watching *The Fast and the Furious*, maybe
10. Without, in Würzburg
11. *City of the Dead* such as the Père Lachaise
12. Greek "H"
13. Visitors from outer space
18. Alfred Nobel or Stieg Larsson, e.g.
21. Consort of Zeus who wound up with a continent named for her
25. Voiced, in phonetics
26. "____ daisy!"
27. Waikiki welcomes
28. A day or two ago, perhaps
29. Joints with caps
32. Famed flautist Jean-Pierre
33. Given a heads-up about
34. "If only that were true!"
35. Sends along an email: abbr.
39. Arctic Circle region rife with reindeer
40. Leg of lamb, in a nice restaurant
46. Marriage announcement
47. Post-pupa insect stage
49. Colorful eye part
50. Part of B.Y.O.B.
51. Gymnast Korbut
52. Peter Fonda's beekeeper role
53. Lays down the lawn
54. Sis's sibling
55. Rocker Ocasek

—

CORRECTION

Words:
George Upton

Video games are not the enemy.

Video games are good for you. Studies have shown that gaming can improve hand-eye coordination, enhance memory and boost visual attention—the ability to interpret what we see around us. The satisfaction of completing a level or mastering a new skill has been shown to contribute to a sense of well-being, and virtual gaming communities have been a vital form of social interaction during the pandemic. Why, then, do video games continue to be blamed for everything from rising rates of obesity and poor academic performance to an increasingly violent society?

Writing in *Psychology Today*, Dr. Tomas Chamorro-Premuzic argues that it has a lot to do with old-fashioned technophobia. Video games fall neatly into a Venn diagram of anxieties often exploited by the media: a mistrust of youth culture and an it-was-better-in-my-day nostalgia for a pre-digital world. But as Chamorro-Premuzic points out, the dangers associated with video games in sensationalized headlines often have their roots far deeper in society—our diets, which have consistently worsened over the past half-century, for example, or cuts in funding for schools. And while people can become addicted to video games, this affects a very limited number of gamers.

The most pervasive myth, that video games encourage violence, has been around almost as long as the games themselves. At its height in the 1990s and 2000s, video gaming was accused of inspiring school shootings in the US, and industry bosses were summoned to the White House. Contemporary research, however, has failed to find any connection between violence and video games, and despite the moral panic, they have never been more popular.[1] In 2019, gamers around the world spent $145.7 billion, far more than box office earnings and music revenues combined. With nearly half of the world's population now estimated to be gamers, it seems increasingly likely that it will be "game over" for the panic.

(1) A 2019 study on the media's portrayal of school shootings, published in the journal *Psychology of Popular Media Culture*, found that video games were eight times more likely to be mentioned as a possible cause when the perpetrator was a white male.

Photo: Gustav Almestål, Set Design: Andreas Frienholt

Words:
Robert Ito

What did *Drag Race* winner SYMONE do with her evening?

Symone, who grew up in the small town of Conway, Arkansas, is the most recent winner of the reality series *RuPaul's Drag Race*. In the competition, Symone was known for her innovative looks including one inspired by the Black Lives Matter movement, complete with Swarovski-crystal bullet wounds, a dress made up of Polaroids of herself and a shapely fox costume.

ROBERT ITO: What did you do last night?

SYMONE: I had some Chicken in a Biskit. You know what those are? They're these crackers you get on the bottom shelf of a grocery store. It's kind of kinfolk to a Cheez-It, but better. So I had some of that, and I watched *Nine Perfect Strangers* with my family.

RI: Who's your family?

S: I'm part of a house called House of Avalon. There's five of us.

RI: What's the perfect night for you?

S: Oh, my God. I am more of a homebody than most people would think. So the perfect night for me is being around my gay family, and us just creating stuff and talking about projects and just being around the people I love.

RI: A lot of people got pets during COVID. Do you have pets?

S: No, I don't personally have a pet, but we have two dachshunds, Fancy and Nancy. I call myself auntie!

RI: Are you a pajamas person? What do you wear to bed?

S: I love a sweat set. So not necessarily pajamas. I like the top to match the bottom.

RI: It's not too hot in LA for that?

S: Not at our house! It's always a meatlocker in there.

RI: Do you ever have trouble sleeping?

S: No, I've never had trouble sleeping. If I really want to go down, I'll go down. But if I do have trouble, I'll watch one of my favorite shows, something comfortable, and then I can just shut my mind off. Like *Charmed*. I love *Charmed*! And *Scandal*, and *A Different World*, and now *The Crown*.

RI: Do you have recurring dreams?

S: No, but one dream that sticks out in my head a lot is, I was Wonder Woman, and I was on top of a roof. And I guess I was just dressed up as Wonder Woman, because I tried to jump and the flying didn't happen and then I woke up right before I hit the ground. I don't know why that dream has stuck with me, but that's the one.

Photo: Max Bronner

SLOW SYSTEMS

Words: Ryan Willms

MANOJ DIAS offers a mini lesson in meditation.

Manoj Dias is the co-founder of Open—a mindfulness, breath work and movement platform—and the author of *Still Together*, a guide to meditation and mindfulness that explores how technology has the potential to compound feelings of detachment. Here, as part of our *Slow Systems* series with Samsung, Dias talks about the importance of breath work and how he gets the best out of contemporary connectivity.

RYAN WILLMS: Tell us a little about Open.

MANOJ DIAS: Open is a mind, body and breath studio, and what that means is that we believe the doorway to mindfulness opens through breath work. Breath work is a prominent part of all the experiences on Open—we integrate it into yoga, Pilates and meditation classes.

RW: Why is breath work so important?

MD: The practice of meditation is really just about coming into contact with reality. And through breath work, we can consistently and reliably enter the present moment. When we come into contact with reality, just as it is, we get to see it, and we get to see what makes us suffer or what makes us happy—and then we have the ability to choose.

RW: What do you personally get out of meditation?

MD: What feels most real and energizing to me is the idea of connection, mainly because it's what I've struggled with most in my life—feeling connected to other people, to myself and to the present moment. Meditation can take you deep inside yourself, but it can really connect you to those around you, as well.

RW: Can it also help you disconnect?

MD: Well, we're connected all the time—we can be connected to our phones and be happy or unhappy. For me, phones can be a tremendous support. I use mine to go to sleep, I use it to wake up, I use it to meditate. I don't think phones are actually the problem; I think it's our relationship to them. It comes down to the heart of mindfulness, right? Mindfulness gives us a choice between stimulus and response, so finding balance is always my goal—knowing when to push and knowing when to pull back. Monday to Friday, I might be going hard, but then Saturday to Sunday, do not reach out to me. Don't email me, don't Slack me, don't text me, don't even think about me.

Photo: Justin Chung. Product: Samsung Galaxy Buds Pro in Phantom Black

STOCKISTS:
A — Z

A	A.P.C.	apcstore.com
	ALICE CICOLINI	alicecicolini.com
	APUNTOB	apuntob.com
	AUGUST LA	augustla.com
C	COURRÈGES	courreges.com
D	DECATHLON	decathlon.com
	DRIES VAN NOTEN	driesvannoten.com
E	EUROPA ART & CO	europaart.co.za
F	FALKE	falke.com
	FINN JUHL	finnjuhl.com
	FRITZ HANSEN	fritzhansen.com
G	GAVIN RAJAH	gavinrajah.com
H	HERMÈS	hermès.com
K	KLÛK CGDT	klukcgdt.com
L	LA COMUNE VINTAGE	lacomunevintage.com
	LE ARTELIER AT BLEND	blendbcnshowroom.com
	LESYANEBO	lesyanebo.com
	LOEWE	loewe.com
	LORENZO MARTINEZ	lorenzomartinezoficial.com
M	MAISON MARGIELA	maisonmargiela.com
	MERWE MODE	merwemode.com
	MISSONI	missoni.com
O	OAKLEY	oakley.com
	OMEGA	omegawatches.com
P	PRADA	prada.com
T	TINA FREY	tinafreydesigns.com
S	SAMSUNG	samsung.com
	STRING	stringfurniture.com
U	URBAN OUTFITTERS	urbanoutfitters.com
V	VIVIENNE WESTWOOD	viviennewestwood.com
	VIVIERS	viviersstudio.com
W	WEDÚ	wedufashion.com

MY FAVORITE THING

Words:
Fernando Caruncho

The garden designer, interviewed on page 92, shares the story behind a painting of his mother.

This portrait of my mother, Sofia Torga, is very special. It expresses her conviction and her purpose in life: the search for beauty through love, discipline and work.

It was painted by a friend of my grandparents called Pedro Bueno—one of the society painters of the time—and I imagine that she must have been around 35 to 37 years old. My mother was born in Seville and lived most of her life in Andalusia. She was brought up in a very particular world—surrounded by culture and creativity—and this, together with her enormous sensitivity and perception, made her a very special person. She was the one who transmitted to me the pleasure of reading, music and a curiosity for beauty. I'm convinced that it was in her parents' house in Ronda, Malaga, that the seed of my future as a gardener must have been planted. She was much loved and admired in her work—she did a great job as a fashion director for 35 years—and those who followed always recognized her as a role model. She had that elegance that comes from within, that is innate, not learned, and it made her a luminous person.

Her children and grandchildren remember her as a very authentic woman—honest and firm in her values—but never forcing anything.

That's why this painting presides over one of the rooms of my studio. I always feel very much accompanied by her presence. In the end, the portrait is a form of landscape, and landscape is the purest expression of the human soul.

Photo: Christian Møller Andersen